Praise for *Brilliant Secon(*

'This book is a godsend for all who are engaged in the education of young people today. Step by step, with easy, accessible, practical tips, each chapter removes the mystique of the journey to becoming a brilliant teacher. Whether you are thinking of becoming a teacher or have been teaching for over 20 years, this book will help you perfect your craft and also remind you why you came into the profession in the first place. *Brilliant Secondary School Teacher* will assist you in the greatest vocation of them all – which put simply is for "education to change lives".'

Alan Perry, Headteacher

'The best advice brilliant teachers can give is strategic – all about how you work out what action to take in this situation with this person right now. Whether you are early or late in your teaching career, wisdom and strategy abound in this easy-to-read book. You'll find yourself thinking: "I do that", and then: "Yes, I'll just try that". What is special about the advice suggested is that it often comes from the authors' own students, which puts a different gloss on the meaning of "listen and learn".'

Dr Malcolm Reed, Senior Lecturer in Education, University of Bristol

'David Torn struggled through one challenging school, achieved success at the hands of inspirational teachers and taught in another. He has gone on to be one of the most inspirational teachers of his generation. Who better then to chart the course for the next generation of young teachers entering our schools today? I welcome this book. His writing is as fresh, his insights as brilliant as the schoolboy I met 30 years ago. He speaks to every staid teacher on behalf of every bored pupil. Here's a book that can make a real difference to teachers' practice.'

Andy I   *of Kingston*

'This book provides detailed insights into the classroom craft of two skilled and experienced classroom practitioners. It gives teachers what they really want: classroom craft with step-by-step instructions and examples. I have been lucky enough to see David Torn performing in the classroom and I have seen him walk the talk. This book will be especially invaluable for new teachers and for everyone involved in teacher induction and training.'

John Bayley, Teachers TV

'I have had the privilege of working with David Torn and Peter Bennett for 10 years. They are both inspirational teachers whose lessons are looked forward to by their students. They have enriched the lives of all they have taught. I cannot think of any better teachers to turn to for advice and guidance on how to interact with students and engage them in their learning. They are looked up to by generations of students and have been influential in the development of many young teachers over the years.'

Ian Raper, Deputy Headteacher

'Wouldn't we all want to be described as a brilliant teacher? This accessible book narrows it down to some core principles; a professional outlook, attention to detail and a belief in young people. The authors have filled the pages with examples of what to do and how to do it, and the detail will help most busy teachers. The belief in young people shines through and the book oozes with professional responsibility. Read the book, take control and enjoy the hard work that helps young people look back on their time with their brilliant teacher.'

Mick Waters, Professor of Education and President of the Curriculum Foundation

'*Brilliant Secondary School Teacher* is a brilliant book! It manages to bring together a vast range of excellent advice and practical suggestions that make it invaluable for someone new to the profession, yet the quality and depth of what's offered means that it also gives renewed inspiration to those who have been teaching for years. Read it, and be inspired!'

Nick Hyde, Director of Science College

brilliant

secondary school teacher

secondary school teacher

What you need to know to be a truly outstanding teacher

David Torn and Peter Bennett

Prentice Hall
is an imprint of

Harlow, England • London • New York • Boston • San Francisco • Toronto • Sydney • Singapore • Hong Kong
Tokyo • Seoul • Taipei • New Delhi • Cape Town • Madrid • Mexico City • Amsterdam • Munich • Paris • Milan

PEARSON EDUCATION LIMITED

Edinburgh Gate
Harlow CM20 2JE
Tel: +44 (0)1279 623623
Fax: +44 (0)1279 431059
Website: www.pearsoned.co.uk

First published in Great Britain in 2011

© Pearson Education 2011

The rights of David Torn and Peter Bennett to be identified as authors of this work have been asserted by them in accordance with the Copyright, Designs and Patents Act 1988.

Pearson Education is not responsible for the content of third party internet sites.

ISBN: 978-0-273-73564-9

British Library Cataloguing-in-Publication Data
A catalogue record for this book is available from the British Library

Library of Congress Cataloging-in-Publication Data
Torn, David.
    Brilliant secondary school teacher : what you need to know to be a truly outstanding teacher / David Torn and Peter Bennett.
        p. cm.
    Includes index.
    ISBN 978-0-273-73564-9 (pbk.)
    1. High school teaching–Great Britain. 2. Effective teaching–Great Britain. I. Bennett, Peter. II. Title.
    LB1737.G7T67 2011
    373.1102--dc22

                                2010053192

10 9 8 7 6 5 4 3 2 1
15 14 13 12 11

Typeset in 10/14pt Plantin by 3
Printed in Great Britain by Henry Ling Ltd, at The Dorset Press, Dorchester, Dorset

Contents

About the authors

David Torn has over 14 years' experience as a secondary school teacher. In that time he has been a very successful classroom practitioner and has led a variety of high-performance teams including a year team, a history department and newly qualified teacher (NQT) and PGCE mentors. At present he is an advanced skills teacher and the professional tutor at St Edward's School in Havering.

As a child David attended Hackney Downs School in East London, which eventually was closed down in 1995 and labelled the worst school in the country, but which taught him the value of education in determining people's life chances. He started his career at St Edward's in 1996 where, after three years in the classroom, he was appointed head of Year 7. In 2005 Ofsted described his leadership as 'inspirational'.

In 2007 David was awarded a PLATO by the Teaching Awards Trust for the London Teacher of the Year. In the same year he won the inaugural GTC Award for excellence in professional development. David is a regular columnist for the weekly newspaper *SecEd* and has worked with Teachers TV on advising NQTs on how to approach their initial lessons.

David lives with his wife Tracy and their two children, Amy and Stuart, in Boreham, Chelmsford.

Peter Bennett was born and brought up in South London. Since finishing his PGCE he has worked in secondary schools for more than 27 years, during which time he has taught nine different subjects and variously been school librarian, a pastoral leader, head of English, gifted and talented coordinator and assessment coordinator. Currently he works as an assistant headteacher at St Edward's School in Havering.

He lives in East London with Monica and a particularly delightful cat.

Acknowledgements

Dave particularly would like to dedicate this book to Tracy for her unwavering belief and support, and Amy and Stuart for finding things to do whilst Dad was writing! Additionally, Helen, Sue, Malcolm and June deserve special mention for their continuing encouragement throughout the project. Pete dedicates the book to Monica, who always showed more confidence in him than he felt was justified.

We would both like to thank all of the people who've had an influence on how we teach and how we think and feel about teaching.

For Dave that's all those who taught at Hackney Downs School in the 1980s and believed that working-class kids were worth fighting for. Thanks also to Sir Paul Grant, who provided huge inspiration during Dave's training at the Robert Clack School and taught him many of the habits outlined in the book, and to all those colleagues Dave has been privileged to work with in the St Edward's history department over the years, most notably Kelly Davis and the current crew – Jon James, Andy McLeod, Rebecca Russell and Liz Wanambwa – as well as his sidekick, Kerry Course. Not forgetting the men that taught him all he knows – Doug Bethell and Martin Jones. Finally, this book is for all those students who have passed Dave's way and proved to be the real teachers.

For Pete that's everyone who used to sit around the table in the staffroom at Carterton when he was training and started teaching, all of the many incarnations of the English department at St Edward's and what must be more than 2,000 students whom he's encountered in the classroom. And, in particular (listed in alphabetical order): Sarah Carr, Andrea Cassidy, Giles Drew, Michael Edwards, Denys Hoyland, Brendan McCullagh, Joyce Nicholas, Anna O'Brien, Helen Rogers, Monica Timothy and Nigel Webster.

In case anyone notices subtle variations in approach from time to time, Dave wrote the introduction and conclusion, and Chapters 1, 2, 8, 9 and 10, and Pete wrote Chapters 3, 4, 5, 6 and 7.

Special thanks to Katy Robinson for putting the idea our way in the first place and providing us with a proverbial kick up the backside when it was required, and to Emma Devlin for organising us and guiding us through the final phases.

Publisher's acknowledgements

We are grateful to the following for permission to reproduce copyright material:

Figure 2.1 from www.learningfundamentals.com.au; Figure 8.1 provided by Mick Waters; Figure 9.1 designed and provided by Burkey Belser of Greenfield/Belser, Ltd.

In some instances we have been unable to trace the owners of copyright material and we would appreciate any information that would enable us to do so.

List of terms and abbreviations

A level	advanced level
AS level	advanced subsidiary level
AST	advanced skills teacher
CAT	cognitive abilities test
CPD	continuing professional development
FFT	Fischer Family Trust
GCSE	General Certificate of Secondary Education
GTP	Graduate Teacher Programme
INSET	IN-SErvice Training
KS3	Key Stage 3 (Years 7–9)
KS4	Key Stage 4 (Years 10–11)
KS5	Key Stage 5 (Years 12–13)
NQT	newly qualified teacher
Ofsted	Office for Standards in Education
PGCE	Post Graduate Certificate in Education
PSHE	Personal, Social and Health Education
SAS	standard age score
SEN	special educational needs
SLT	senior leadership team
ST	student teacher
TA	teaching assistant

Foreword

The role of the educator in our society must never be underestimated or undervalued. It is, to my mind, the most important of professions. It is also, as I have only too sadly realised in recent years, a profession that is constantly under the microscope and that constantly attracts the often misguided comments of society. In this country, too many people spend their time bashing teachers and criticising standards.

These people are, almost always without exception, ignorant of the work that happens in our schools, ignorant of what it takes to inspire a child in education, and ignorant of what good teaching looks like. I spend every day of my working life trying to champion the cause of teachers and my message is incredibly simple – you, as a profession, know what you are doing and how to teach every child effectively, so believe in yourself. You will always have the carpers and cynics who stand on the sidelines and criticise, but it is not these commentators, politicians, journalists or even Ofsted inspectors that you should listen to.

The only people you should listen to are your fellow professionals – to those who 'get it'; those who understand how important the profession is to our society; who understand the many and varied societal factors that every child can bring with them into the classroom; who understand that some days are just plain difficult and there's no escaping the fact; who understand how to get through to every child and give them as best a head start for life as they can.

David Torn and Peter Bennett are two of these teachers. They 'get it' and the guidance and advice in *Brilliant Secondary School Teacher* – a vital book – is invaluable to the new teacher and, I would contend, provides an always welcome refresher for those more experienced at the chalkface. The breadth of skills it takes to be a good teacher is awe-inspiring. The challenges that teachers face every day in the classroom are endless – planning effective lessons, managing behaviour, dealing with parents, ongoing continuing professional development (CPD), inspiring and educating children with many different learning styles and abilities, the list goes on, as well you know.

And new teachers must realise that, more so than in most professions, the life of a teacher is one of constant development and constant learning. It is okay if some days you struggle. This is natural, but with the support of your fellow professionals, with their guidance and advice, you will succeed.

David Torn and Peter Bennett have been fighting the good fight for years and their passion for education, which in David's case can be found in his regular column in *SecEd*, to me sums up how the profession should be.

Their advice is the most crucial – advice to tackle those everyday issues that every teacher worries about, such as planning and teaching effective lessons, engaging all learners, assessment, use of emotional intelligence, meeting a class for the first time and even dealing with homework.

There is no getting away from the fact that the challenges that educators face can be daunting, especially for new teachers. But we are lucky to have teachers of David's and Peter's calibre in schools across the country, and it is these professionals who will play some part in helping our young teachers to develop, and the circle of education will always continue.

So this is my message to you. Believe in yourself, believe in your profession – you are the ones who 'get it'. And when you take advice on board make sure it is not from the politicians, the cynics and the carpers on the sidelines; make sure it is from those within the profession who 'get it' and who believe, like you, that education truly saves lives. *Brilliant Secondary School Teacher* will help you on your journey in doing just that.

Pete Henshaw
Editor of SecEd *and* Delivering Diplomas

Introduction: reminding ourselves what is important

At a pinch you might be able to do without parliaments, you could do without the ministers: you could certainly do without civil servants and most certainly without local education authorities. Without any or all of them the world might not seem much worse. But if there were no teachers the world would return to barbarism within two generations.

George Tomlinson

S tudy after study has revealed that the single most important factor in deciding a child's education is the quality of the teacher they have. *The purpose of education is to change lives.* It is about ensuring that every child really does matter and that the life chances of every student are maximised. For some, teaching comes naturally and is instinctive but for the vast majority of us we have to learn how to teach. The aim

> the single most important factor is the quality of the teacher

of this book is not only to give you practical advice on all aspects of teaching, but also to remind you continually of why you became a teacher in the first place – *to change lives.*

What makes a brilliant teacher?

This is the one question that all new teachers want to know the answer to. What is it that differentiates the ordinary teacher from the extraordinary one? A very useful exercise is to ask the students themselves. Even disaffected students will come up with what they see as the qualities of an effective practitioner and they are usually the same qualities that teachers value in effective students! Brilliant teachers genuinely believe in the youngsters they teach and this comes across in every classroom every day. They are passionate about their subject and are able to transmit this. Brilliant teachers are excellent at giving praise but equally good at showing when they feel disappointed by a student's performance; they are able to communicate their emotions very clearly. They are fantastic at developing *relationships* and see this connection as a pivotal factor in the student's success. In addition to this, whilst brilliant teachers take others very seriously they do not always take things to heart. They have a sense of humour and in this profession the ability to laugh at yourself is vital.

> in this profession the ability to laugh at yourself is vital

Lessons are carefully planned and organised so that learning is fun and discipline is secure with students feeling physically and emotionally safe in the class. Although brilliant teachers are likely to be individualists they will also recognise the contribution of their colleagues in promoting a team ethos. However, perhaps the single most important characteristic of the brilliant teacher is *expectation*. These are the teachers that believe that all of their students *are* capable of achieving and consistently inject a *'can do'* attitude into the youngsters they work with. And, as Zig Ziglar (an American motivational speaker) put it, they continue to reinforce the notion that 'it is attitude, not aptitude that determines one's altitude'.

Why do we need brilliant teachers?

In September 2007 a landmark report on worldwide education was launched – the McKinsey report. The report highlighted the fact that the single most important factor that determined a child's education was the quality of the teachers they had. In almost every country educational reforms remain top of the agenda. In 2006 alone the world's governments spent over $2 trillion on attempting to bring about educational reform. Despite this, 780 million adults in the world remain illiterate and every year another 100 million join them. This report was followed by a 2009 documentary entitled 'We Are The People We've Been Waiting For', which further examined the education systems across the world and asked why some countries were more successful than others. In Britain alone 30,000 youngsters leave school every year with no qualifications whatsoever. Sadly, it is still very much the case that where you are born and the environment into which you are born strongly determine your future success in education and, indeed, later life.

One of the key findings of the McKinsey report was that a student placed with high-performing teachers will progress three times as much as one who is placed with low-performing teachers; research shows that the impact of poor teaching on students is such that, where students encountered poor teachers over a prolonged period, the educational loss is almost irreversible. Despite this, some schools in Britain have defied the odds and shown that by investing in teachers and developing them as practitioners extraordinary results can be attained. These schools have shown that a student's background is not always a viable explanation for underachievement.

> by investing in teachers extraordinary results can be attained

Three main factors can be identified in relation to what the best schools do and why their students achieve:

1 They are meticulous about getting the right people to become teachers in the first place.

2 They are very serious about providing them with high-quality continuing professional development (CPD) in order for them to become effective practitioners.

3 They are insistent that every child receives the best possible education.

This is where you come in. The purpose of this book is to complement the training you may have had already and to provide you with the best possible practical advice that we can. *It is not a quick fix.* You need to be serious about being a brilliant teacher and to recognise that success lies in developing good habits. The purpose is also to encourage you to seek that special something that makes you stand apart in the classroom.

We would encourage you to read the book in its entirety if you want to get the most from it. However, it can also be used to give you advice on developing certain aspects of your current practice. We have included a collection of brilliant tips, examples and case studies should you want to have a quick skim read. Nevertheless, it is important that you acknowledge that becoming a brilliant teacher is not an overnight process and will require that you practise the advice offered with regularity and reflection.

> becoming a brilliant teacher is not an overnight process

If you are entirely new to the profession, you should find that the book is full of useful advice that will make your life easier. Similarly, if you have taught for many years, the book will serve to reinforce what you are already doing and to refresh your practice. We hope that you are enthused about what you read and that you continue to see teaching as the highest calling there is.

Finally, this book is not a book for now; it is a book for always because teachers affect eternity – nobody knows where their influence ends.

Good luck on your journey to becoming a brilliant teacher.

CHAPTER 1

The journey to becoming an outstanding teacher

To me the sole hope of human salvation lies in teaching.

George Bernard Shaw

As the quotation on page 1 says, brilliant teachers are saving humanity! But the journey to becoming a brilliant teacher may not be as hard as you think. It is certainly not rocket science and there are a variety of techniques that brilliant teachers use that will help you to get the best out of the students you teach. Most of the chapters that follow focus on sharpening the way in which you approach certain aspects of teaching. You will, however, find it easier to apply these approaches if you have a strong notion of what students perceive a brilliant teacher to be.

This first chapter will examine the characteristics of brilliant teachers and provide a basis on which to build. It will give you clear advice on what students are looking for and what they are certainly not looking for. The schools of today are markedly different from their predecessors and we can be sure that schools will keep on changing, but good teaching will continue to be based on the relationship between the teacher and the learner. Don't misunderstand the implications of this, though – there is rigour involved, too. We know that some groups in British society tend to be less successful in school than others and it's important that the teacher is consciously aiming to make sure that *all* students achieve as highly as they can. The warm glow of a positive relationship also needs to produce learning!

We will then move on to examining the key features of high-quality lessons with a particular emphasis on the need for tasks to be challenging as well as accessible.

First things first

'No one forgets a good teacher'. You may remember that this was the slogan used not so long ago in a series of TV ads to recruit new entrants into the profession. And it is true – no one does forget a good teacher. However, what does it mean to be a 'good teacher'? Is it just someone who regularly meets the core teaching standards or someone whom Ofsted judges as 'outstanding'? The most effective way to find this out is to speak to those who really know and who matter most – the students. They will tell you exactly what they see as a 'good teacher' and, interestingly, you can almost guarantee that the perception of a good teacher will be consistent from student to student. Additionally you will get *honest* feedback; it will not be couched to make you feel better or wrapped up in coded language. Students are astute and will tell you unambiguously what their understanding and expectations of a 'good teacher' are.

'no one forgets a good teacher'

brilliant tip

Brilliant teachers are *always* looking to improve and be the best they can. They are *not* driven by the latest initiative or the current thinking of Ofsted. They simply want to ensure that every student gets the best possible deal. As a result they are always open to new suggestions from students and are not afraid of honest feedback. (If you are committed to being the best you can, you must be prepared to hear things that might make you a little uncomfortable.) If you want to be a brilliant teacher then ask the students, 'What makes a good teacher?' You can do this in open discussion or by using questionnaires. However, if you use discussion it is extremely important that the ground rules are laid, such as ensuring that subjects and teachers remain anonymous. In their first week in our school, PGCE or GTP students are encouraged to approach students in the playground and ask them, 'What makes a good teacher?' This is then used as a basis for discussion in their initial mentoring session. Year after year the PGCE students return with the same answers. It is important for teachers to listen to the students but, more importantly for *you*, the ingredients for being a 'brilliant teacher' are right in front of you. Go ahead and ask them!

Ordinary or extraordinary?

Think carefully about this question: by the end of your career what impact do you want to have had on the lives of the students you have come into contact with? You know what it is like when you get together with old school friends and discuss your school days. There were the teachers you did not warm to because they seemed apathetic towards kids and there were some you cannot even remember because they appeared to lack personality and passion. However, there were ones that everyone remembered for the important reasons. The ones who were passionate about their subject. Of greater significance they were interested in you and transmitted an attitude which made everybody believe it was possible to achieve. These were the ones that made an everlasting impression and we have no problem in admitting we want to be remembered in a similar way. When students are reminiscing about their school days we want to be the type of teachers that they felt believed in them and enabled them to meet their potential, and we want to be remembered in the same way, not because of ego but because this is what teaching is about – providing the opportunity and conditions for all to reach their potential.

The characteristics of brilliant teachers

The great thing about what follows is that the evidence suggests becoming a great teacher is not beyond the reach of any practitioner who is willing to listen to and act on advice. So, if you are reading this and telling yourself that you will never be a brilliant teacher – *think again*. Over the years research has gone into finding out the *habits* of successful teachers and they always come up with the same results. The good

---
perseverance is the key!
---

news for you is that below is a list of these characteristics followed by a short summary for each. If you were to practise these consistently there is no doubt that you would be well on your way to becoming a brilliant teacher yourself. Remember – perseverance is the key!

1 *Brilliant teachers have high expectations and believe in the students they teach.* This is one of the key factors in educational attainment across the country – *high expectations*. Consider why groups of students do well at school. It is often because of social conditions and the fact they are brought up to believe success is possible. Some have parents who are professionals and, having attended university themselves, expect this for their children, but very many students come from a background where there is low educational attainment perhaps coupled with low expectations. The teachers who monitor their students effectively, identify underachievement and put measures in place to tackle it are often the ones that students remember most. These teachers do not see background as an excuse for failure, though they may recognise it as a factor contributing to low self-esteem. Additionally, great teachers do not see success as age-related. For example, it is not that unusual for students who are gifted and talented in a subject to tackle GCSE or even A-level work when they are in Year 8. What pervades all of this is a *'can-do'* attitude which recognises student potential and is also realistic. This brings to mind the story of the teacher who, when faced with a student stating that they could not do it replied, 'You are quite right. You cannot do it ... yet!' The message

here is to believe in everyone you meet. You may be the one who makes the difference.

2 *Brilliant teachers maintain high levels of discipline and are good role models.* A teacher who can control the class very often will be at the top of a student's list of favourites. Students want to learn in a safe environment and are looking for the teacher to set the tone. It may sound surprising, but even the most disruptive of students are looking for clear boundaries and they will continue to create problems until they know where they stand. This is why it is essential that teachers lay the ground rules in the very first lesson so that students know where their boundaries are (more about this in Chapter 2). Brilliant teachers recognise that effective discipline is the cornerstone of good teaching and without it no one can produce imaginative lessons. Though it can be daunting, do not shy away from outlining your expectations for behaviour at the earliest opportunity. Moreover, good discipline does not mean shouting but quite the opposite. As with the lesson content good behaviour needs to be planned for and is the subject of Chapter 4. If you want students on side, model good behaviour – show them politeness, patience and respect, as well as communicating that you like them!

3 *Brilliant teachers are very explicit in what they are teaching and how it will be assessed.* These are the teachers who have detailed lesson plans so students know precisely what they are meant to be learning. The learning objectives are clearly shared and students have the opportunity to practise new skills. Subject knowledge is excellent and students feel secure that they will be making progress during the lesson. Work set is meaningful and the teacher communicates to the class the purpose of the task. When homework is set it is marked with diagnostic feedback giving them useful advice that will allow the student to make progress.

Students like to be given the opportunity to assess their own work or that of their classmates as it allows them to understand where they are. The same principle applies in many walks of life. You would not pay for driving lessons in which the instructor did not provide opportunities to practise your learning – the same applies in the classroom.

4 *Brilliant teachers make learning exciting.* Highly effective teachers are adroit at making seemingly boring topics interesting. They are enthusiastic about their subject and communicate this to their students. They use technology in an inventive way. They also create tasks that get students engaged and give them time to think about what they are learning. Students are given time to try out new things and get things wrong because so much learning takes place by being allowed to make mistakes. Often lessons begin with a question or a puzzle and students are 'hooked' early on and are so engaged that they do not even realise how much they are learning.

5 *Brilliant teachers see relationships as the key to successful learning.* The best teachers we know are passionate about their students and show that they are interested in them as individuals. They are warm, approachable, caring and enormously enthusiastic about those in their presence. You need to show that you are interested in your students and, rather than avoiding tasks such as break or lunch duties, embrace them as opportunities to get to know students outside of the classroom. This is a very powerful way of engaging with students that you cannot do otherwise. It is also essential that you are prepared to give students a 'fresh start' if there has been some tension in previous lessons. One of the interesting responses that students give to what makes a good teacher is one who does not hold grudges. In fact it is extremely evident that, until you have some kind of relationship with the students in front of you

(and that may be as simple as knowing and using their names!), you are not teaching them anything. You may think you are, but the reality is that you are merely sharing information. Great teaching requires great relationships. To read more on this particular aspect look up *The Craft of the Classroom* by Michael Marland, an OBG (an oldie but a goodie).

6 *Brilliant teachers are seen as fair and have a sense of humour.* Students have a keen sense of right and wrong and are looking to be treated fairly. In your day-to-day career it is highly likely that you will get things wrong for one reason or another. For example, you might accuse one student of chatting when, in fact, it was the person next to them. Having the courage to apologise and admit to the student (or the class) that you did get it wrong is an impressive quality to have and will reinforce the students' positive image of you. Moreover, be prepared to laugh at yourself, using humour positively. Being able to make others laugh is a fantastic way of easing tension and making the learning experience that bit richer.

7 *Brilliant teachers are team players.* Experience has taught us that the very best teachers appreciate being part of a team and recognise that success comes from close collaboration with colleagues. Being an effective teacher is not about being the best teacher in the school, a *prima donna,* full of self-importance. Great teachers are more than happy to share their resources with members of their team and, indeed, to receive the ideas of others just as openly. See cooperation as the key to success for all students and go out of your way to cultivate staff relationships within and outside your department. It is when people start believing that they are too important for the team that things go wrong; don't let success go to your head – the need to keep a sense of perspective is crucial.

8   *Brilliant teachers are great learners.* Perhaps, most importantly, the best teachers believe that there is always something new to learn and are continually open to suggestions. They recognise that no matter how much experience they have, there is always room for development. They are not interested in new initiatives for the sake of them, but will be interested in assessing how they can develop their own practice. More importantly, perhaps, is that effective teachers allow themselves to make mistakes and look to learn from them, just like they expect their students to do. Failure is instructive in itself and, if you see it in this way, you will learn as much from your failures as any success you might have. You need to have this frame of mind if you are to develop into the best that you can be. The old saying that the more you learn the more there is to know is an appropriate one to remember. Recognise that success is a journey, not a destination.

 **example**

A prime example of someone who continually looks to improve is the Olympic 400-metre gold medallist Christine Ohuruogu. After securing gold at the Beijing Olympics in 2008, Christine was asked how she felt. Rather than whooping with delight, she enquired whether her performance was a personal best. Obviously it mattered that she won the race but, more importantly, she was interested in continual self-improvement. She recognised that there is always room for improvement and this is the same with brilliant teachers. Success has no ceiling.

Just what do effective teachers do?

Even the best teachers will have days when things go wrong and some lessons are lousy. However, successful teachers generally are able to teach highly effective lessons day in and day out and recognise the need to update their skills continually. They plan in depth and constantly reflect on their practice. If a lesson has been particularly successful in the past there is no guarantee that this automatically will be the case again. In that sense they never assume and are always looking to teach a subject in a new or different way. It is to the area of planning that we must now turn our attention. Though we will explore lesson planning further in Chapter 3, what follows is an overview of the ingredients of successful learning and why some colleagues consistently shine.

> successful teachers plan in depth and constantly reflect

What makes learning successful?

Successful schools primarily rely on what happens in the classroom. One of the main messages of the McKinsey report of 2007 was that a school's success could not exceed the quality of its teachers. When planning any lesson, make sure you consider the following aspects. Whilst these may be common sense, it is surprising how many lessons fail to include one or more of them. Read the following list of dos and don'ts and think about your own practice.

brilliant dos and don'ts

Do

✔ Have a clear and explicit learning objective – have this written on the board for the students to copy and ensure the word 'learn' is included. For example, 'Learning objective: *to learn why Hitler came to power in 1933*'. You are communicating to the students that, by the end of the lesson, they will understand the main factors that led to Hitler's accession to power.

▶

✔ Have a starter activity that encourages students to think. It does not always have to be related directly to the topic, but it helps. (See more about these on pages 14–15.)

✔ Include two or three activities that you can explore fully for a lesson that is 50 minutes or an hour long. It is no good having five or six activities that you can only skim over.

✔ Build in mini plenaries after each activity. Use them to ascertain what students have learnt from them and to refer back to the learning objective.

✔ Explicitly give timings during the lesson and adapt them if necessary ('You now have five minutes to go').

✔ Use praise regularly and acknowledge when a clear effort is being made.

✔ Notice when students are off task or disrupting and intervene early to deal with it. (More about classroom management in Chapter 4.)

✔ Design tasks that are engaging, challenging and that encourage students to think.

✔ Build discussion into the tasks. Designing pair or group work where students have to share their opinions maximises student participation and minimises the need for students to talk unnecessarily. Remember that when students are engaged in a task they do not always have to be talking – for every speaker there should be at least one listener!

✔ Set homework early on in the lesson. Even if students do not fully understand the task when you set it, by the end of the lesson it should be clear.

✔ Seek feedback on your teaching. Students will be honest and tell you what went well and what needs improving. Possibly uncomfortable, this is nevertheless a really effective way of finding out how your students learn and what they enjoy.

Don't

✗ Be afraid to seek advice from other professionals in the classroom (e.g. TAs) as they may be able to tell you what works with particular groups of students.

✗ Always follow your lesson plan to the letter. Sometimes the lesson might not go in the way you planned, but students may be learning effectively. Go with the flow!

✗ Assume that because you have taken hours planning your lesson materials every student will automatically understand the tasks. Have you built in differentiation? There's more about this in Chapter 7.

✗ Take it personally if things go wrong. Continually reflecting on successes and failures is an important part of improving your teaching.

↗ brilliant case study

Alison is a teacher at a mixed 11–18 comprehensive school. She is now in her fifth year of teaching and is head of department. From the moment Alison began teaching she willingly listened to and acted upon advice. As a newly qualified teacher, Alison ensured that lessons were planned meticulously and always with student progress in mind. Despite being one of the school's most successful teachers, Alison never takes anything for granted. Lessons are still planned with the same rigour and take account of the dos and don'ts outlined above. As a result, Alison is not only an outstanding practitioner, but is also a fantastic role model for other colleagues in the school.

In the beginning ...

One of the key questions to consider is, how do we encourage pupils to focus on their learning within the first two minutes of walking into the classroom? It is important that students are on task as soon as possible so that maximum engagement can take place. The other consideration is, how do we reinforce learning? This commonly is known as the BEM principle (beginning end middle). The idea is that students learn more effectively at the beginning and end of a lesson rather than the middle. Therefore, delivering worthwhile starters and plenaries should not be something that is done for the sake of it, but because there is educational value in them.

> students learn more effectively at the beginning and end of a lesson

brilliant tip

Engaging learners as soon as you can is an excellent way of minimising off-task behaviour and allowing students to get 'stuck in' right away. The most effective teachers are aware that disruption is more likely to take place when students are not engaged. Designing interesting and stimulating starters can also give you time to take the register and settle students down.

Some instant ways to engage learners

- *Just a minute!* Choose one person to stand up and speak for a minute on any topic you desire (if students were learning about circulation in the previous lesson, for example, they could recap their knowledge). The aim of the game is to encourage one student to speak for a minute without stopping. If they hesitate or fail to reach a minute you can select another person. This is fantastic for recall and works best when three or four students are involved.

- *Odd one out.* Students are presented with a series of words or images on the board. The odd one out should not be totally obvious, and the task should allow students to discuss a variety of options. Students could do this in pairs and share their thoughts with the rest of the class.

- *Hidden image.* This is a version of the 'Magic Eye' puzzles that were popular about a decade ago. It works best with an interactive whiteboard or even overhead projector. Students are shown an image and asked to work out the hidden image within it. You can find examples of these by typing the term 'hidden images' into an internet search engine.

- *Thunks.* These are brainteasers developed by Ian Gilbert in *The Little Book of Thunks.* Some of the examples include, 'Is a broken down car parked?' or 'Is there more future or past?' They are fantastic ways of getting students to think outside the box and engage in debate. Again, you can find some of these by entering 'Thunks' into a search engine. These work with all age groups, perhaps especially Key Stage 5. They can be used to get students to discuss the Thunk in pairs for 30 seconds and then explain their reasoning, or to get students involved in lengthier debates.

As well as those discussed above, there are numerous ways in which to begin a lesson that provokes engagement. Some teachers have a picture on the board ready to discuss, others have subject versions of game shows such as 'Deal or No Deal'. Whatever you choose to do, try to vary it from lesson to lesson. What seems exciting in one lesson could become boring if overused!

The key thing to remember is that you are engaging students in the thinking process immediately and can then move on to the next part of the lesson. By getting students 'hooked' you are already on your way to delivering a successful lesson. It is not the intention here to explore the topic of structuring and planning high-quality lessons (see Chapter 3 for this), but it is important that the basic principles of successful learning are made clear from the start.

The end game

As much as it is important to engage learners at the outset of the lesson, it is equally vital that the end of the lesson has the same impact. Useful plenaries will be beneficial in that they will allow you to reinforce the message of the lesson as well as gauging how much learning has taken place.

Suggestions for plenaries

- *Tell your friend.* This is a paired discussion in which one person tells their partner three things they have learnt this lesson and vice versa. When the teacher goes to that pair they repeat what each other has learnt. This is an effective way of diagnosing whether the desired learning has taken place or not.

- *What if…?* This is an activity that students can undertake on their own. Give them a minute or two to consider what they have learnt today and to write it down at the back of their book. They can also add what else they would have liked to learn. When you take their books in to mark you will be able to see what they have said.

- *Traffic lights.* Students are given three cards – red, green and amber (students often have these in their planners). The teacher can remind them of aspects of the lesson and ask them to show their understanding. If they fully understand it, they show green; if they get it partially, they show amber; if they do not have a clue, they show red. One way to tackle this is to get the greens to talk to the reds whilst you talk to the ambers. This is also a good system to employ during the lesson itself. However used, it allows you to assess the effectiveness of your lesson.

- *Mark my words* (especially good for Key Stages 4 and 5). Students are given the criteria and encouraged to peer assess a classmate's work. This is particularly effective for exam-based questions or developing a particular skill.

There are hundreds of ideas you can gather from other colleagues or books and then use or adapt. The important question to ask yourself is, 'Have my students left my lesson understanding more than they did last lesson?' Remember, all of this is a learning process and you will find things that work with some classes, but not with others. And don't be afraid to take risks – it is vital that you learn as much as those in front of you!

 brilliant recap

- Aspire to be the best you can – why be ordinary when you can be extraordinary?
- Talk about the qualities of an excellent teacher to those who matter most – the students!
- Find out who the most effective teachers in your school are. Ask if you can observe them and see what they do in the classroom. So much can be learnt by observing.
- Build up a bank of starters and plenaries. Remember not to rely just on technology: you may be in a room without an electronic whiteboard.
- Take risks and do not be afraid to get things wrong. In developing the humble light bulb, James Watt was asked how it felt to fail so many times (apparently it took him over 700 attempts to get it right). He replied that he had never failed but found 699 ways of doing it differently!

Summary

The final factor to consider is optimism. Teachers, by definition, need to be the ones who encourage and see the positive in every situation. Apart from parents, teachers are the most important adults in a child's life. Students are looking for you to be consistent in your approach. You really are in the most rewarding profession there is. In what other walk of life can you be the person who gives shape to the life of another individual? Students will remember the teachers who always encouraged them and cultivated within them a 'can-do' attitude. You are instrumental not only in their subject learning, but also in how they come to view life itself. In an ever changing world, shaping a positive attitude is as important as any knowledge that you will teach them. With this in mind it seems appropriate to leave the final words to Alexander the Great: 'I am indebted to my father for living, but to my teacher for living well.'

CHAPTER 2

Starting afresh: early contact with classes

To climb steep hills requires slow pace at first.

William Shakespeare

Every September you can bet that many of your colleagues will joke that, during the six-week break, they have forgotten how to teach. The reality is, however, they are not joking! No matter how much experience you have acquired, the beginning of a new school year is always one of trepidation and anxiety. Getting off to a good start is essential in ensuring success for the rest of the year. Overwhelmingly we have found that the teachers who spend time at the beginning establishing routines and expectations are the ones who face the least difficulty in the classroom later on. This chapter explores the importance of setting ground rules early and creating high expectations. Alongside this, the need to learn students' names as quickly as possible and develop relationships will be discussed as well as first lessons with A-level students. The key thing to understand is that what happens in the early stages largely will determine the progress of teacher and class during the following nine months or so.

Who do you think they are?

As will be discussed further later, schools are data-rich institutions and you might well find yourself inundated with information regarding your students from day one. As well as class lists, you will be provided with data relating to special educational needs (SEN), ethnicity, Key Stage 2 results, Fischer Family Trust (FFT) data, along with a plethora of other information that might or might not prove relevant. You could even be lucky enough to be given photographs of the students! If this is the case you are already in a good position to get to know their names before you meet them for the first time. If the students are in Year 8 or above you could well hear about their reputations from colleagues – 'Not them. I had them last year and they were the worst class I have ever taught!' Or, 'You will be fine with them. I certainly had no problems.' Teachers often like to give labels to students and classes but these kinds of comments are not always helpful because they may create a false impression.

Whilst you should be aware of the data you are provided with, it is important to remember that data does not really provide answers, it merely serves to raise questions. In a study in 1984 Ted Wragg, a noted educationalist, found that the more experienced teachers often began by making sure they had the essential medical information about students, such as deafness or epilepsy, and little else. They preferred to find out about the students themselves before looking up any records on their character or background. The main difference between then and now, of course, is the availability and variety of data, and both your head of department and the SLT would expect you to have much of it in your markbook. In short, however, the more experienced practitioners tend to use data more as a guide than as infallible truth and seek to avoid any preconceived ideas before their initial encounter with any new class.

Toeing the line

The impression that you create when you meet a class for the first time is one of great significance. Over the last century a number of social psychologists have conducted reviews of first meetings between people and the interaction that occurs between them. One of the key features of the various research is the speed at which individuals reach conclusions regarding the person they meet. Teachers that have worked in a particular school for a period of time almost always have an advantage over those who are new. Reputations may have spread amongst siblings and students will often know what to expect before they even arrive at the class. Experienced teachers arriving at a new school will need to re-establish themselves in their new surroundings, but they at least have more of an idea of how to do this than their newly trained colleagues. The way you dress, your manner and your ability to assert yourself will all play a key role in the way students respond to you over the next academic year. Often a key difference between teachers that get off to a solid start and those that do not is the expectations that are set out at the very beginning, something we will look at closely later in the chapter. Below are some key tips that will allow you to get to know your students quickly as well as to assert your authority.

brilliant tips

- Before students enter the room ensure any equipment they may need is already placed on desks. This includes exercise books and any handouts that they will need. Also ensure that your name and title is written clearly on the board along with any other relevant information such as subject, room and the name of the class. This makes it much easier when they come to write these details on the front of their books.

- As the students enter your class for the first time, be at the door as they file past you. Not only are you in a position to greet them in a positive manner but also you can pick up immediately on such things as uniform and chewing gum. You might even want to be holding the bin so that students know you mean business straight away.

- Ask the students to line up against the wall so that you can place them in their seats. Some teachers have a seating plan on the board so that students can find their own places. The problem with this approach is, if you are a new teacher or the class are particularly difficult, it could prove disastrous early on. Getting them to line up so you can place them is an early way of asserting your authority.

- Seat the students according to some plan, such as in alphabetical order either from the back left to right or from the front. Whatever way you choose, placing them alphabetically in the first lesson allows you to find out who's who as early as possible, as well as sending them a signal that you are running the class. Some teachers like to seat students alphabetically boy/girl/boy/girl which, again, is fine. The main point is that you should place them. You will undoubtedly meet colleagues who find this unnecessary and allow students to sit where they like until there is a need to move them. These will often be the teachers who are already well respected in the school and have no need to assert themselves. However, in conversations we have had with NQTs and second or third year teachers at the end of the first half term, many express a wish that they had placed students themselves at the very beginning and state their intention to do so at the beginning of the next half term!

- Do not worry if you find that you have not taught much during the first lesson. Getting across your expectations and aspirations will prove more beneficial to you in the long run. You will find that experienced teachers are not too concerned about what is actually taught in the first lesson, but that they have set clear boundaries and ground rules. If you do manage to teach them something, make it as dramatic and interesting as possible. Communicating a passion for your own subject is important, and if you do not seem interested in it, how do you expect them to be?

What's in a name?

The most effective way to establish control from early on is to know the students' names. It sounds obvious, but when you first meet 25 or so new people you might not remember all of their names straight away. Moreover, if someone has their back to you, the chances of getting them to turn around are far greater if you can

> knowing students by name from as early as possible will prove invaluable

say, 'Excuse me, John ...' rather than, 'Will you turn around.' Knowing students by name from as early as possible will prove invaluable. There are many ways to learn names including the suggestion below.

 **brilliant** activity

During your first lesson challenge the students by telling them that you will be able to remember their first name by the end of the lesson. Offer 10 pence to any student whose name you cannot remember. Throughout the lesson constantly memorise the students' names until you are entirely confident. Use the plenary to go around the class naming each student. Have some money ready just in case you have to pay up, but by placing them in alphabetical order you should already be in a strong position. Additionally, you might already have photographs of the students in which case it will be a breeze. If you do have access to their photographs beforehand, why not create cards with the students' names on the back? This way you can regularly test yourself! Most importantly, though, the students will appreciate the effort made to get to know their names.

Great expectations

The most important message that you should seek to communicate in the first lesson is the expectations that you have of the students. These should cover all aspects including equipment, homework and classroom conduct and you should stress the positive as well as the negative consequences. It is also an opportunity to dispense with any negative labels the class may have. Taking time to go over this in depth will not only save you time later on, but will also ensure that firm boundaries have been established. Failing to do this in the first lesson could mean that your expectations become compromised. The programme 'Tough Love' on Teachers TV (www.teachers.tv/videos/tough-love) gives you practical ways of explicitly doing this. Finally, this is your chance to set the tone for the rest of the year. Whilst you do not want to come across as an 'easy target', the importance of creating an open learning environment cannot be overemphasised.

 **brilliant** activity

Look at the list below and consider how serious you see each point in terms of affecting the learning of others. Rank order them from 1–5 (1 being the most disruptive to learning and 5 being the least). Once you have done this, consider what your sanctions are going to be and whether they are in line with departmental expectations. Ask yourself whether they are realistic or not and we will then give you suggestions as to what we see as reasonable. Remember, you need to be aware of these from day one so that you can communicate them to the students. Having a clear knowledge of the rewards and sanctions will also help with consistency and create a safe learning environment for the whole class.

(a) Turning up without exercise book/textbook.

(b) Non-completion of homework.

(c) Constantly disrupting other students.

(d) Shouting out.

(e) Challenging the authority of the teacher.

Turning up without exercise book/textbook

During the first lesson set firm rules about this. For Key Stage 3 students, if they forget their book once, put a code in your markbook (b: book or nb: no book). The second time they forget their book, a detention should be issued. You need to decide on the length of the detention (long enough to have an impact but not so long as to be unreasonable and cause resentment), but whatever you decide you must follow through. Every time it happens after this you should set a detention. This might sound harsh, particularly if the student is in Year 7, but soon you will discover that the majority of students will always bring their book, and you will not have to chase students up to mark work or constantly hand out paper. You may well have students with organisational difficulties, in which case it is worth you holding on to their book and using your common sense as to how you administer this sanction. For students in Key Stage 4, remind them of the rule in the first lesson, but make it even tighter. Tell them that as soon as they forget their book once it will result in a detention. Again, there will be colleagues who will say this is unworkable and that it will be impossible to enforce and, admittedly, it will require determination and effort on your part. Our answer to this is to ask how serious you really are about raising attainment. Once students realise that words are hollow and the consequences are not clear, it will be increasingly difficult to enforce your expectations.

Non-completion of homework

First, ensure that homework is used to set meaningful tasks or students will not take it seriously anyway. Having said this, expectations should be made clear from the start. For non-completion of homework apply a sanction straight away and this should be made clear in the first lesson. You need to decide what the sanction is and for how long and, unfortunately, it will take up some of your time and patience. However, it is equally important for you to remind yourself that you are establishing the ground rules and you should expect them to be challenged by students quite early on. As with the forgetting of books, there will be exceptions and

> all effective teachers need to be flexible

you will need to use your common sense. All effective teachers need to be flexible, but at the same time setting high expectations from the outset should be seen as a key priority.

Disruptive behaviour

In order to address issues of disruption, such as the ones listed in c, d and e above, it would be a good idea to have clear rules that all students are expected to adhere to at all times. The simpler they are the more effective they become. It also helps if all teachers are following the same expectations. The two rules below, for example, are very basic, but cover all eventualities.

1   Do as you are asked first time without arguing.

2   Do not speak while the teacher or other members of the class are speaking.

↗ brilliant case study

Martin was in the second year of his degree and went back to his old school to visit one of his teachers. In fact it was the teacher of the subject he had chosen to do at university, history. The conversation soon progressed to how Martin was doing and what he hoped to do once he had graduated. Before he left he shared a secret with the teacher. 'Do you know one of the reasons I am studying history at university?' he asked. 'Tell me,' replied the teacher. 'In our very first lesson in Year 10 you told us that if we forgot our book once we would get a detention, and you communicated to us the importance of the subject. You were so passionate about the subject that we could not help but become enthusiastic ourselves. After the lesson, not only did I want to avoid detention but I also wanted to learn more about history.'

Obviously it was not just the discipline that Martin bought into. He enjoyed the subject and, perhaps more importantly for his choice of university course, was successful in it, but the very clear guidelines ensured he had a safe environment in which to work. Therefore it is extremely important to set very high and clear expectations from the very first lesson. With this in mind it is also vital that you set a tone of optimism. For many of the students it may be the first time you will have taught them and for others the first time they will have seen you! You need to create a purposeful atmosphere in which students will want to invest time and energy in learning your subject. It is equally important that you get a message across to all students that learning will be interesting and their views will be valued. Creating this sense of balance will prove significant in the weeks and months ahead.

The language of positivity

Putting across a positive message will establish high hopes as well as expectations early on. Some classes will turn up at your door with a bad reputation and others with a good one. It is important that you transmit positive vibes as soon as possible. Use phrases that will encourage the students to work with you rather than against: 'I'm really looking forward to working with you this year. I have heard so many good things about you and have every confidence that you will live up to your reputation.' Or if they

> transmit positive vibes as soon as possible

come with a health warning: 'By the end of this year you will be the best class in the year group. This is a fantastic opportunity for you to prove to me and yourselves that you can achieve at the highest levels.' Remember, students want a teacher who is calm and in control and who will offer them the chance of achieving.

As well as laying down clear sanctions tell them what you will do to celebrate achievement. It might be that you have taken over a class where expectations are low and students that work hard are made to feel embarrassed. In this case it is even more important to break the cycle of underachievement and apathy. We would advise that you make it a priority to get the message across to the class (in particular the negative peer leaders) that the game is up and from now on praise will be used effectively to reward both good behaviour and hard work. Take a moment to think about how you are going to celebrate achievement. Look at the list below and see if you can add to it.

● Genuine and positive praise in front of the class.

● A letter or a phone call home to inform the parents/ guardians about the pleasing progress X is making.

● Displaying work in the classroom.

● Selecting a student of the month (you decide on the criteria – the wider the better) whose name and reason for selection will appear on a noticeboard for the rest of the class to see.

Whatever you decide to do it is of the utmost importance that you stick to it. As with the sanctions you have decided upon, students will work out very quickly if you are genuine or not.

---

brilliant example

Sarah was an extremely bright Year 9 student in a mixed ability English class. At the beginning of the year the class were known for having been particularly difficult throughout the previous year and were determined to live up to this label. By October the class had written their first extended essay and Sarah's was especially good. The teacher decided to praise Sarah publicly and it was evident that she was not happy about this. Gradually, as the teacher grappled with behavioural issues and the class's own perception of themselves started to change to one of positivity, so Sarah's own attitude towards success and public recognition changed. By the end of the year she was continuing to write essays that bordered on ones that A-level students would have been proud of. The main difference was that it was now a good thing to achieve. Note, though, that when the culture of the class had been 'anti-intellectual' Sarah was not willing to go against the grain. This is why it is of central importance that the teacher sets the tone and sticks to it. The reality is that, in some cases, three or four students will have a stranglehold on the rest of the class and the 'silent majority' are desperately hoping that they will get a teacher who has the courage of their convictions and is willing to take on the ringleaders as well as celebrate achievements on a regular basis.

Share something about yourself

Though it may sound somewhat risky so early on, students can often relate to a teacher more if they see them as something more than an authority figure. Sharing personal stories and having the ability to laugh at yourself is often a good way in and can break the ice. There is also no harm in establishing your own credibility. Sometimes this will happen automatically as siblings or older friends of your students pass on stories concerning your reputation. Otherwise, letting students know about prior work experience, travel or research you may have undertaken enables them to have more confidence in you and adds to your own credibility.

What to teach ... if anything?

As already emphasised, the aim of the first lesson is to set the tone for the rest of the year. Establishing ground rules, devising seating plans and beginning to develop relationships are the key priorities. However, if you do have a spare 10 or 15 minutes, try to capture the imagination of the students. Do something that will appeal to hearts and minds. This may sound cheesy, but this vital first meeting provides you with an opportunity to re-enthuse their attitude towards learning. In fact, you don't even have to teach them anything about your subject. It may be about learning in general. In Chapter 1 we recommended using Ian Gilbert's *The Little Book of Thunks* to engage

> do something that will appeal to hearts and minds

learners in conundrums. Sometimes using an image or part of an image to invite discussion is a good idea, as are cardsorts. However, whatever you choose to teach, think big and choose something that will leave them wanting more.

Preparing for first lessons with post-16 classes

One of the biggest areas of stress for new teachers, and even those with some experience, is how to prepare for the first time they teach a lesson at Key Stage 5. Quite often it may be the case that the age gap between a young teacher and the A-level class is relatively small. Some teachers feel they can relax more with an A-level class, and in some respects this is true, but it is vital to remember that you are still the authority figure, and there will be a need to establish ground rules from the very start. These may be to do with work patterns and, in some cases (admittedly very few), it might be necessary to have a seating plan worked out. If this is the case, it is far better to establish this early on than leave it until the third or fourth week. Getting students into good habits and behaviours does not stop at 16!

Again, think about how you are going to conduct this first class. There will not be as much of a need for the emphasis on discipline as in 11–16 classes, but setting clear parameters is still a necessity. With post-16 classes (as with GCSE) it would be a sensible idea to give the students an overview of the specification as well as showing them what the actual exam paper looks like. Remember, post-16 students will have only two and a bit terms to complete the course so letting them know early on what to expect is to their benefit. Other ways to engage them are suggested below.

● *Famous people in …* Whatever subject you teach there will be a wealth of famous people associated with it. Whether it be mathematics or fashion you could get the students to think about 10 famous people associated with your subject in one minute. For example, if you are studying the history of modern Italy they could cite painters, politicians, etc. Alternatively, for business-related courses they could mention modern figures such as Lord Sugar as well as medieval Italian bankers such as Filippo Borromei. When they have completed this task you can then give them a list of 10 famous people in the field and the things for which they were actually famous. Make this a mix and match exercise, which gets them to think about the answers. A great way to get students into a new course!

- *Mind mapping.* Another effective way to start is to communicate to the students the importance of study skills, using mind maps as an example. Either a mind map produced by you of the course or one made by the students of their current knowledge is a good way to start the course. Figure 2.1 overleaf illustrates one way in which this can be achieved.

- *Discussion cards.* Again, this will be related to the subject you teach. Take a variety of key words or phrases (perhaps 20 or so). Get students to work in pairs. One person has a minute to discuss what the key term or phrase means and then the players swap. The object of the exercise is to encourage discussion as well as to introduce students to new words and concepts.

Whatever you choose to do, think carefully about how you are going to communicate expectations with the content of the course. What you do in the first lesson will very much set the tone for the rest of the term and so, whether you are teaching Year 7 or Year 13, be very clear in what you want from them as well as where you are going.

Remember, you certainly will not be the only one in this position in September; every teacher you know will have a strategy or plan that deals with opening lessons. Although teaching can often seem like a lonely profession, most of your concerns are shared by others.

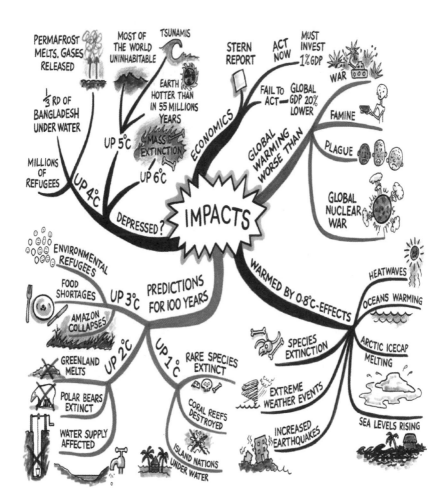

Figure 2.1 Mind mapping

Source: www.learningfundamentals.com.au

 recap

- With any new class make your expectations very clear. Do not be vague as to what will be tolerated and what will not.

- Use the first part of your lesson to seat your students and go through the expectations. Do not worry if this takes longer than expected.

- Seek to learn names as soon as possible. This is the most effective form of control.

- Share your hopes as well as laying your ground rules. Students are looking to you to be optimistic about their future.

- If you do get on to the teaching have tasks that are stimulating and provoke debate. Your aim is to have them leaving the class wanting more.

- Do not assume that post-16 students will just 'get on with it'. You will have to share your expectations with them as well.

- Be assertive! You might be really scared and as nervous as anything. This is fine, as long as you don't show it! The art of coming across as confident even when you are not is something perfected by all teachers. For many teachers there is a lot of truth in the words of Franklin D. Roosevelt in his inauguration speech – 'The only thing to fear is fear itself'.

Summary

Starting the right way is important. It takes longer to correct things than it does not to do them in the first place. A little extra effort establishing expectations at the beginning will help you to teach better and students to learn more quickly in the following months.

CHAPTER 3

A class act: planning exciting and highly challenging lessons

It's a poor plan if you can't modify it.

Publilius Syrus

E very teacher is unique, as is every class and every lesson. Learning in schools involves a lot of people who are in complex relationships with each other, and that means you can never predict with certainty quite what's going to happen and how students (or teachers) are going to react. That's why a sensible and flexible approach to planning is so important: you may not know quite what is going to happen when

a sensible and flexible approach to planning is so important

you light the blue touch-paper but you need to have clear ideas in your mind about what you *think* you are going to be doing and what you *think* might result, as well as having some responses ready if everything doesn't go quite according to that plan.

Don't teach lessons that dogmatically stick to the plan, even when it is clear that everything is going pear-shaped, and don't cut short productive digressions that have been raised. And, if we talk mostly about planning and preparing, please don't understand that as us saying that only learning that you have anticipated and are in control of is valuable. Paddy Creber (author, lecturer and teacher trainer) once wrote that good teaching has a strong element of interested experiment about it, with the result that good teachers often don't know quite what they are doing! This isn't a charter for not preparing, but it is a reminder that creative teaching (and learning) happens when we are operating at the limits rather than in the comfort zone.

Advantages and disadvantages of planning

Good lessons need to be planned but there needs to be a sense of practicality about that planning. The demands of some schools for *evidence* of planning has created a perception that this is an onerous and bureaucratic task, something that is done to pacify managers, not a creative activity that enables you to do the best job you can. Planning doesn't have to involve time-consuming filling in of detailed sheets, but it does require thought so that you take into account the needs and abilities of the class that you will have in front of you. Similarly, the passive adoption of someone else's scheme of work without any consideration of how easily the lessons will fit with your style and personality, and with the needs of your particular class, isn't really planning. Creative planning may well take an established scheme of work as a starting point but it will need to be reviewed critically in order to make sure it allows you the best possible chance to help your students learn. The best teaching is individually tailored, not off-the-peg!

At its worst, planning takes up hours of teachers' time, writing down detail that is inappropriate and unnecessary. It can impose a strait-jacket on thinking, kill spontaneity and lead to formulaic teaching. At its best, though, planning leads you to imagine new possibilities, to use resources efficiently and effectively and to have a reference point for reviewing the lesson.

---

brilliant example

As an example of what to **avoid** it would be hard to beat this beginning of a lesson plan that a student teacher prepared:

- Say 'Hallo, class'.
- Wait for reply.
- If no reply, repeat 'Hallo, class'.

- Ask, 'Did you have a good weekend?'
- Wait for reply.
- Ask two people what they did at the weekend.

And so it went on for pages. This isn't a plan – it's a script! And, of course, the class sullenly refused to respond to 'Hallo, class' no matter how often it was repeated. The whole lesson had been planned in similar detail (with timings, measured in *seconds* in some sections). It is hard to describe quite what a stultifying and dull lesson resulted from this meticulous planning that paid no attention to the realities of a secondary school.

Planning needs to take account of the long-term and medium-term aims (What subject content do I want to cover with this class this year? What skills do I want to introduce or reinforce this term?) and needs to build on what you know about the students, either from their primary schools, in the case of Year 7s, or from their previous teachers and the school records in the case of other year groups. Give yourself the flexibility to adjust your plans when you get to grips with the reality of teaching a class. It may be that you need to reinforce a skill (the class that struggles with group work, for example) or that a concept that is essential for future progress just won't sink in and takes more time than you had budgeted for, so have

> give yourself the flexibility to adjust your plans

some ideas about how you might modify your plans. What is essential and what could be sacrificed if push came to shove? Never forget, though, that your decision to change your plans may have implications for others in your department, particularly when resources are scarce. There are few things more annoying for others than being told on a Monday morning that the materials they were relying on won't be available because you haven't finished with them after all. Other people mustn't be made to pay the price for your flexibility.

Don't think that writing everything down in enormous detail is a guarantee of success; thinking everything through will probably be of greater benefit. Yes, it can be really helpful to have some rough notes and some indications of timings for the various parts of the lesson (in surveys of students, they rate having variety in lessons as a feature of good teaching), but writing down too much takes up a lot of time and can lead you to file away the lesson plan to be recycled without further thought or adaption. After all, you planned it once, why reinvent the wheel? Not giving enough thought to your plans for a class will prove disastrous, but too much detailed written planning can lead to fossilisation of your lessons, so beware!

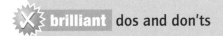 **brilliant** dos and don'ts

Do

✔ Have a plan of your intentions for the year and for the half term.
✔ Take account of resource implications within your department.
✔ Make use of departmental schemes of work, but customise them.
✔ Spend as much time as you can thinking about what you might do, how you might do it and how it all went.

Don't

✗ Plan in minute detail – it's not necessary and can get in the way of learning.
✗ Take other people's plans and use them without thinking about how they need to be modified to suit you and your class.

Planning for pace

Plans don't necessarily have to be written down but lesson plans need to be clear in your mind from before the lesson starts. Resources have to be prepared, for example, or groupings for oral work decided. You need to have got the balance right between pace and learning – too fast and more and more of the students don't understand, too slow and more and more students stop paying attention. You need to know what you are going to do if some students finish early, and what you must keep in mind all of the time is the general principle: do less, learn more. Don't cram in so much activity that nothing ever quite gets finished or the frenetic pace results

do less, learn more

in stuff getting done but no one ever having time to reflect on what it all means. Better to have five minutes at the end of the lesson that you can fill with one of your favourite standbys (and if you don't have a range of impromptu five-minute activities, start collecting them now!) than to leave things unfinished and the class confused.

brilliant tip

A timer or stopwatch can be incredibly useful to keep you on track. Most electronic whiteboards will let you have a timer on the board (although at times this can be too intrusive) but your mobile will have a timer or you can buy an electronic one from a kitchen shop. For writing activities, say, where you want students to spend 15 minutes, you probably don't want them to have an eye on a giant timer when they should be writing (the time becomes more of an issue than the task). A small timer that you see and they don't works well here. You can give updates – 'Five minutes left' – to keep a sense of urgency, and there is something very satisfying about the beep of a timer signalling the end!

Many teachers find it hard to get a sense of what can be achieved in a given time and the basic rule is, it always takes longer than you think. Allow more time than you think you'll need the first time you do an activity and then use your experience and skill to adjust your expectations in future. How important is it that everyone reaches the end of an activity? Very weak students often can manage in quite tight time frames (they don't see all of the possibilities that the more able do) but in many lessons a large proportion of the class never actually finishes anything. If you find this happening you need to have more open-ended activities and you should allow more time for each activity, having prepared an extension task for the early completers.

Another danger to watch out for is not leaving sufficient time for actually assessing whether or not students are learning, so be sure you've planned for when and how you are going to check that; 'I taught it to them but they didn't learn it' is not something you want to find out weeks or months after the event! Better to cover less content and ensure learning happens than to do all that you had planned with many of the students having learned nothing.

A colleague once told us about the two teachers he had had for A-level maths. One was by far the superior mathematician but she struggled to see things from the perspective of her students, who weren't as gifted as she was. If anyone had the temerity to say they didn't understand something she repeated herself, more slowly and louder. If they still didn't understand, she moved on regardless. The other teacher would try to explain things in a different way and, if that didn't work, he would try another different way. The pace was slower in his lessons but people learned things.

Planning for structure

There's something of a fetishistic attitude towards the three-part lesson in some quarters, as if somehow or other the mere presence of a starter and a plenary (or of things that get *called* a starter and a plenary) makes or breaks the effectiveness of a lesson. It doesn't! Some of the least effective lessons we have seen have had a rigorous three-part structure and some of the most effective didn't. It's a very useful planning tool and structural device but no more.

Starters

Ideally you want your lesson to capture the interest of your students from the beginning – that's where a good starter can come into its own. You also want to establish how the lesson fits into the bigger scheme of lessons and you may well need to accommodate the trickling in of students who are coming (with varying degrees of rapidity!) from different parts of a large site. Having the starter activity outlined on the board or already on desks is ideal if you are teaching in a classroom, as it lets everyone get going as soon as they arrive. A puzzle of some kind

> capture the interest of your students from the beginning

or a quiz that requires knowledge of what happened in previous lessons will do the job, as will getting students into pairs to recall the key facts about the topic you are working on. This is also the time when students who have been absent can be helped to get to grips with what they've missed (by getting other students to recap the missing lessons for them) and when you can chat to the early birds.

Some starters have problems in that they go on for too long or they get truncated by teachers who are desperate to stick to a rigid time scheme. Think about what you want to get out of the activity and budget your time accordingly. If you've got a great idea for an open-ended task that you suspect will work best at the beginning of the lesson, don't arbitrarily stop it after five minutes because that's how long you feel a starter ought to last for. Ask yourself how worthwhile a task is and then give it the time it deserves. Also, think about why you are using this particular starter activity at this particular point in a scheme. Make it clear to students if it is an activity unconnected to what comes next – you know it's just a starter but they think it's part of the lesson and some will get themselves confused when you move on to the main part of the lesson.

brilliant example

Starters may look back, stand alone or look forward. Here's a fairly random list of effective starters that we've seen in use that builds on the very general suggestions in Chapter 1. How many can you tweak so that they will work in your subject?

- *Recap (in drama).* Students talk in pairs to see how much they can recall of what they did and why in the previous lesson. The teacher then reconstructs the lesson and the learning but asks students (no hands up!) about what went on.

- *Quiz (in science).* Students work individually on a quiz about the previous lesson and then check answers in pairs using their exercise books and textbooks for information. The teacher then puts up the answers on the board and moves the lesson forward to develop the topic.

- *Puzzles (in English).* Students work in pairs on lateral-thinking puzzles. After five minutes the teacher goes over the answers with them.

- *Discussion (in religious studies).* Students work in pairs discussing a moral dilemma that is displayed on the board. After five minutes or so the teacher picks three individuals to summarise what they think.

- *Vocabulary test (in modern foreign languages).* Students match words to pictures to reinforce vocabulary relevant to the topic they are working on.

Plenaries

Badly executed plenaries are truly dreadful but an effective plenary is extraordinarily useful! The badly executed plenary usually is perfunctory, squeezed into the last few seconds of the lesson and superficial. At its worst the teacher says, 'What have we learned today?' and a student recites back the lesson objectives for the teacher to agree with.

The best plenaries have a proper amount of time devoted to them and let students think for themselves about what they have learned. They allow for self- and peer-assessment, short tests, performance and analysis, getting students to make a list of a couple of pieces of knowledge they acquired and a skill they practised, target setting, making an entry in a learning journal and so on. Remember, rather five minutes to fill at the end of the lesson than a rushed and unsatisfactory conclusion.

brilliant tip

A really simple but effective plenary is to put students in pairs or threes and get them to agree between themselves what they thought they learned during the lesson. You can add extras to this, such as asking which part of the lesson they most or least enjoyed, what they think you should do differently if you were to teach the lesson again, which part of the lesson they think they would most benefit from going over again, and so on. Give them a few minutes and then pick out random students (not volunteers, and keeping a record of whom you asked helps you to make sure that everyone gets picked out at some stage) to give you answers. You can help develop things by asking why they feel as they do or by asking other groups if they agree or disagree with the point that's just been made and why. Everyone gets to reflect on the lesson and you get some useful feedback.

Planning for creativity

Teachers, like students, tend to be very conservative creatures, never happier than when things are happening in the old familiar way. Anyone who has ever tried to initiate change in school knows just how hard it is to alter people's engrained habits and approaches. Electronic whiteboards, for example, are frequently used to display PowerPoint presentations which students copy down, just as in the past they copied from overhead projectors or from chalkboards – the technology has moved on but the pedagogic technique often has shifted very little from when we or our parents were at school.

Creativity can be stifled by too strong a conviction that a lesson should be composed of a number of discrete sections building up to a neat and straightforward learning objective that can be summarised in a few words. Risk taking is not something that has been encouraged amongst teachers or students, but let's remind ourselves of Paddy Creber's dictum about good teaching involving experiments in learning – if we are going to extend our students and ourselves, we need to take risks.

> to extend our students and ourselves, we need to take risks

One way to do this is to try to use more open-ended tasks or tasks that can be completed in a range of ways. Take a topic that you normally teach in a conventional way and collect together a range of resources on it. This needs to include written material that ranges from the very straightforward to the very advanced. Make provision for internet access for at least some lessons. Now put the class into groups, mixing the students up so that they are forced to work with at least some people who aren't from their usual friendship groups.

Explain that you want each group to prepare material to teach the topic to students about three years younger than them (as you well know, teaching something to younger people means you really have to understand it). Each group needs to produce, for example, four or so sides of A4 on the topic, in general, and a poster and a brief video to explain a specific aspect of it. You could leave the group to decide on the specific aspect or you could decide on the aspects and distribute them yourself. Each group needs a leader who is responsible for making sure that everyone has clearly defined tasks, including homework tasks and deadlines for completing work. Each student must make at least some contribution to the writing and have a part of the final product that is identifiably theirs.

Keep in mind that the class almost certainly will need to spend more time on the activity than first thoughts would have suggested (but insist that everything must be completed within the time frame you specify). If this is the first time you have done something like this, be prepared for a degree of apparent chaos. One skill that teachers regularly fail to demonstrate is leaving students alone so they can get on with things without constant interruption and correction. After the start, when you recommend resources with appropriate degrees of challenge to different students, be interested in what's going on, offer help and advice when it is asked for (although refusing to intervene can be a good strategy), throw in provocative questions, but don't interfere more than you have to. If things are not being done how you would have done them, step back. Let students develop their own methods and make their own mistakes. Try to avoid giving answers if things start to crash and burn but instead help students come to their own conclusions about why things aren't working and what they need to do to get things back on track. Lean on the group leader if individuals in their group don't appear to be pulling their weight.

At the end you need to be sure that you give time for exhibition and presentation (voting for the most successful poster, say, introduces a competitive edge that might, or might not, be a good strategy with your class) and for students to reflect on what went well or less well in their approach to the task. Do not just have a plenary about what they learned in terms of content. It's a situation that is tailor-made for really effective peer-assessment (see Chapter 5).

> ### 🟊 brilliant tip
>
> Try limiting the availability of the most desirable resources to encourage planning and focus. So if students get access to the video camera for only one lesson, and they have to have a script and know where the scenes are being filmed before they get a date for filming, they will be much more organised about getting things prepared.

Often it is these kinds of lessons that stick in students' memories and that deepen their interest in a subject. Many students will go the extra mile when the task is open and there are great opportunities for differentiation – not many students can resist if you tell them that the resource you are recommending to them is extremely challenging but you think that they'll be able to cope and that they could then explain it to the others.

We're not claiming that this is the only way to be creative but as an approach it's flexible, allows work to be personalised and often is a great motivator.

> ### 🟊 brilliant tip
>
> When you find a technique or approach that works for you there's a temptation to overuse it, so be aware of the need for variety. The cleverest technique can become routine very quickly, both for you and for the students, and you don't want to get to the stage where you are going through the motions. Give it a rest sooner rather than later.

Planning for skills

Think back to your own days at school: how many lessons do you remember? Chances are there are whole years when you can't even recall who it was who taught you or what it was you learned. Some lessons or parts of lessons will still be memorable (often for the wrong reasons – a science experiment going wrong, an awful injury in PE, a teacher breaking down in tears in the face of poor behaviour) but the vast majority of your education washed gently over you. No doubt a lot of the knowledge from those days faded pretty quickly, but what you surely gained at some point in your education was skill at locating information and evaluating its usefulness.

Too often we assume that students already possess sophisticated skills but many potentially effective tasks fail because our assumptions are wrong. 'Research' homeworks produce nothing more than some cutting and pasting, usually from only one source and the first thing generated by the search engine; group work degenerates into chatting and rowing; open-ended questions are closed down and dealt with perfunctorily. As with so much else, teachers need to be explicitly teaching skills to students and then giving them the opportunities to practise them. And all this needs to be planned in advance.

Group work

Ted Wragg was Professor of Education at Exeter University for many years. In his book *Classroom Teaching Skills*, he told the story of a student teacher watching the regular class teacher at work, the kind of teacher who makes the whole thing look effortless. A week later the ST takes the class, imitates exactly everything the regular teacher did and chaos ensues. The lesson for teachers is that what looks effortless usually isn't. The strange thing, though, is that experienced teachers will still treat group work as if it were simple and self-evident. We'd suggest that not many teachers pay enough attention to teaching the skills that students need in order to become competent at working in groups and,

what looks effortless usually isn't

once again, there needs to be planning to integrate these skills into lessons.

Individuals will have their own strengths and weaknesses when it comes to doing group work but classes have their own dynamic as well. By encouraging self- and peer-assessment you can help students develop their individual skills, and by setting up varied tasks and by experimenting with different ways of organising students you can learn how to get the best from the collective and about where the weaknesses are that need to be worked on.

 case study

7Z was a mixed ability class and they could not get on together. Any kind of group work would break down fairly rapidly. Some students would refuse to work with certain other individuals: one would pointedly turn his back on the group, another would cry! Chatting was rife, with a general belief that group work meant talking and not necessarily on the topic set. Written tasks usually were well done, the class could settle and follow text-based work and class discussion wasn't *that* bad, but group work ...

As a consequence, the plan for the year had to be revised to increase the amount of talk. That was the weakness and so it needed addressing. First of all most talk was done in pairs, with the partners regularly swapped about and a record kept of who brought the best out in whom. Some students could work effectively with anyone, some with no one and most needed to be matched up with the right individuals.

The types of task were varied too. Tasks usually were brief but might be problem solving, word puzzles, attempts to find practical solutions to problems, talk about abstractions ... Feedback was from individuals chosen by the teacher, and if someone was unable to give feedback they would be warned that next time they would be chosen again to ensure they knew that active participation was not optional.

In a spirit of 'interested experimentation' larger groups would be constructed randomly, of mixed-sex pairs, of combinations that *ought* to work, or of combinations that surely *wouldn't* work. Some lessons were chaotic, but slowly things improved.

The drill for moving into groups was worked on – no one was to move until all of the groups had been read out or displayed on the electronic whiteboard, if the room had one. All movement was to be completed in one minute at most. Groups were to sit in a cluster not in a line. If possible, groups of four were to rearrange the furniture so that they sat around one table, close together, not staring at each other at a distance across two tables.

Individual students were encouraged to organise where they sat more carefully (for example, Liz must always have her back to Sue and be at least half a classroom away from her; Jeff needs to be in the middle of the group to keep him paying attention).

Tasks ended with peer- and/or self-assessment. A record sheet of group-work skills was used and students were asked to focus on developing skills such as the ability to make accurate notes, to provide summaries of what had been said before, to change their minds as a consequence of discussion or to stick to their guns if they were sure they were right. Students realised that they had skills they were unaware of (being good at encouraging others to speak, for example) or weaknesses that needed to be addressed (not being assertive enough when they knew they were right).

It was a long year but, at the end of it, there had been achievement because of long-term planning to address a weakness and lots of planning of varied tasks and different groupings.

Thinking skills and problem solving

Often as teachers we are too concerned with content and end product, with the result that we lose sight of the valuable learning that happens in the process. The regular complaints amongst teachers about students who expect to be 'spoon-fed' and who are unable to think for themselves are unwelcome testimony to the ways in which teachers have taught them. Students need opportunities to develop their own thinking and study skills, but if lessons are over-prescriptive then those opportunities will be denied to them. That's why longer-term plans must be constructed to include space for students to work on tasks in which they can develop thinking skills. As we said above, letting go of control can be a frightening prospect for many teachers – but it doesn't need to be. The edginess that comes from not quite knowing what is going to happen can help us understand why Ken Weber, the Canadian educationalist, described teaching as the most exciting thing you can do with all of your clothes on!

And before someone misunderstands us, let's be really clear: we've nothing against knowledge or teaching students so they end up with factual information in their heads. We aren't setting up an either/or situation – knowledge _or_ skills – we're saying that you need to be planning for _both_ knowledge _and_ skills.

> you need to be planning for _both_ knowledge _and_ skills

You may be clear in your own mind that most of your subject involves problem solving. That's wonderful if it's true, but you want to make sure that you are making the most of those opportunities and identify areas where you could increase the challenge for students. We often believe that we are doing something until, under scrutiny, it becomes apparent that actually we aren't doing it as much as we had assumed.

brilliant tip

In his wonderful book _Irrationality_ Stewart Sutherland devoted a chapter to how we (unconsciously) distort or ignore evidence to make it fit in with our plans and beliefs. Constantly review your plans and look at the evidence with as open a mind as you can. Do test results suggest that the class _really_ understands a topic? Have they *really* mastered a skill? Our inclination is to see things as supporting what we would like to be the truth so it takes a deliberate effort to make ourselves evaluate the evidence in a more open-minded way.

There are many great sources of ideas for helping students develop their thinking skills. The books of Edward de Bono feature a number of thinking 'tools' like Plus, Minus and Interesting (PMI) or Six Hats Thinking, which can be used with just about any age or ability students. PMI involves taking a proposition and listing the advantages and disadvantages that follow from it, together with any more tangential thoughts that it provokes. Used by small groups of students, it can be adapted to any subject's content and, by limiting the time for the brainstorming of each of the three elements, can be done as an effective starter. The starting point can be fairly off-the-wall and then often will generate some more practical ideas.

Here's a PMI exercise that has worked well with mixed ability Year 7 classes, as well as with older students. You give them three minutes to come up with plus (P) ideas, three minutes for minus (M) ideas and three minutes for interesting (I) ideas. It's important that they learn not to discuss the ideas at this stage – they need to generate as many thoughts as they can, good, bad or indifferent! Once a range of ideas are generated they can be evaluated and discussed.

---

brilliant example

What if the school stopped providing chairs in each classroom, but instead required students to buy their own folding chair, which they had to carry around with them from room to room?

Year 7 students came up with the following thoughts.   ▶

Plus

- There would always be enough chairs for everyone in the class.
- You would look after the chair more carefully because it was yours.
- It would be easier to keep the floors and tables clean without chairs in the rooms.

Minus

- The corridors would get more congested between lessons.
- The chairs would have to be stored somewhere at the end of the day and at lunchtime; people might steal other people's chairs.

Interesting

- Get rid of desks and tables too.
- Students could decorate and customise their chairs.
- People could hire themselves out to carry other people's chairs.

Students grasp the principles quickly and then it's the teacher's job to look out for opportunities to encourage the use of this way of thinking. A colleague of ours has assured us that her brother had actually used PMI to decide whether or not to marry his girlfriend. Clearly a thinking technique with great possibilities in the real world!

 brilliant recap

- Planning is something that teachers do in order to help students learn. It isn't something they do in order to keep line managers off their backs!
- Effective planning requires more thought than it does ink.
- Other people's plans almost certainly will need adjusting in order to fit your style of teaching and the demands of your particular classes. Your own plans that worked with

one class won't necessarily work with another class without adjustment.

- Your plans are only plans – they should be varied and adjusted to take account of the situations that arise.
- When planning timings remember that everything always takes more time than you think it will.
- Most students don't acquire or develop skills without the teacher planning for this to happen.

Summary

Picture a swan gliding over the waters of a lake: serene, unruffled, tranquil. We can't see under the water but if we could we'd find its legs were going like the clappers to propel it along. A lot of invisible hard work is creating the effortless quality the swan projects.

When you are in the classroom, surrounded by students learning, you may well make the whole process appear effortless. A visitor would imagine that there wasn't much to this teaching lark but you know that, under the surface, it's your planning for learning that is propelling the whole thing along!

CHAPTER 4

Know the golden rules: managing the class effectively

They have bad manners, contempt for authority, disrespect for older people. They no longer rise when their elders enter the room. They contradict their parents, chatter before company, gobble their food and tyrannise their teachers.

Socrates

S ocrates had it right. It is not only you that has had to deal with stroppy behaviour. It has been the norm amongst our young (and indeed some of our elders) since time began! The issue is, how do we deal with the undesirable behaviours and encourage the ones we approve of? In fact we'd go so far as to say that discipline is the starting point of success in the classroom – if the class won't sit down, won't listen to instructions and explanations,

> discipline is the starting point of success in the classroom

won't attempt tasks, then learning is not going to happen. Not being able to keep discipline is also, without doubt, the biggest concern amongst most teachers near the start of their careers and amongst a lot of teachers who've been doing the job for years.

In Chapter 2 we explored the approaches you might consider when taking over a new class. The aim of this chapter is to allow you to develop and fine-tune the habits and skills that will, in the main, enable you to manage behaviour successfully in order to give all students the best possible chance of learning to their full potential.

What do students want?

So, what do students think makes a good lesson? Take a few minutes to think this through and jot down what the responses would be. And, while you're about it, what do students think makes a lesson poor?

Over several years the senior staff at the school in which we work regularly asked students from Year 7 to Year 11 these questions. At first their replies were collated and analysed but, after a couple of years, we found we were getting nothing new to add – the consistency from year group to year group and from year to year was scary! Have a look at what we found in the following case study – see what you'd anticipated and what surprised you and, particularly, look at what they had to say about teacher behaviour.

Children want to feel safe and they want to know that someone is in charge of the situation. They won't be hurt, they won't be intimidated because Ms X is in control of the room. She's calm, she's relaxed but she won't allow anything bad to happen. We all know a Ms or Mr X – we may even have been lucky enough to have been taught by her or him! The class could do exciting stuff because the teacher was in charge and confident enough to allow risk taking, and the students could offer opinions and try things out in a secure environment.

What happens when the teacher isn't in charge? The lessons will tend to be more focused on trying to keep students quietly occupied, there'll be no activities where there's potential for chaos (which often means that students get bored quickly) and the stress levels will be high as the teacher over-reacts and tries to enforce a level of control that is beyond them. Who would want to be in that lesson either as a student or as a teacher?

brilliant case study

A wide range of students of both sexes and aged from 11 to 16, interviewed in single-sex groups of three, were asked what made a good or a bad lesson. The results have been tidied up to remove repetition and so some are in 'teacher-speak'.

Good lesson

- Variety of tasks which are fun.
- Work pitched at the right level – challenge but not too difficult.
- Some active work involved (especially chances to do drama!).
- Gets students involved and gives them opportunities to express their own opinions.
- Responsive to students' interests and enthusiasms.
- Well organised with extension work available if you finish early.
- Rewards for doing well.
- Lots of enthusiasm and support from the teacher.
- Teacher has control; the teacher is calm and relaxed.

Bad lesson

- Pace is too fast – no chance to practise what's being taught.
- Not enough challenge.
- No variety of activity.
- Not much chance to be creative.
- Poor class behaviour.
- The teacher doesn't make it fun.
- The teacher is always shouting.
- The teacher has little control.
- The teacher talks all of the time.
- The teacher is moody(!)
- The teacher doesn't listen/the teacher makes you cry.

Note how the teacher was almost invisible in the 'good' lesson and there was nothing about students being well behaved. From a student perspective, good behaviour is a bit like water to goldfish – you notice it only when it isn't there and then its absence is catastrophic! The students' perspective seems to be that the teacher sets the tone for the lesson.

▶

If you aren't convinced, try collecting your own data; it isn't difficult – all you need is 30–45 minutes, a quiet room and a group of about three students of the same age. Single-sex groups work well and allow you to explore whether there are significant differences between boys' and girls' expectations (we didn't find that there were and found that poorly behaved boys had remarkably similar expectations to well-behaved girls).

Our point is that the control you manifest in the class is crucial and that almost all students want you to be in charge. They may challenge you but they don't really want to win!

Know yourself

Relationships are at the centre of behaviour management – the students behave for *you*. This means that you have to develop a sense of who you are and what your limitations are. As Guy Claxton said way back in 1978, when he was lecturer at the University of London Institute of Education, 'Learning to be a teacher is not just learning a new job – it is a new way of being yourself.' Some techniques will work for other people and not for you, and that's fine because you'll find some approaches work for you and other people wouldn't find them effective. Having a repertoire of behavioural management techniques can only be good but slavishly trying to do things that just aren't you will be disastrous. And what works with one class won't work with another, and the same with individuals. The teacher who is brilliant at behaviour management will adopt different approaches with different classes and students while all the time recognisably being her or himself.

> develop a sense of who you are and what your limitations are

brilliant tip

Don't set yourself up to fail. Work around problems rather than confronting all of them head on. For example, some people can make the rowdy class stand silently behind their chairs, and most of us can't. If this approach just isn't you (not least because after 15 minutes the lesson *still* hasn't started) do it differently. Start with an activity that gets everyone working on their own, or in pairs, as soon as they arrive in the room. Now you can pick up issues with individuals rather than getting into an 'And I say you will and they say they won't' stand-offs. You've got them engaged from the start and now you can move on in the lesson without beginning with conflict.

A senior member of staff once had to deal with an issue when a parent brought in a complaint about the way a teacher had treated her son. As the story unfolded it became apparent that the teacher hadn't actually said anything that the senior teacher hadn't also said to that child. When this was pointed out the child explained, 'It's all right when you do it because I like you.' You couldn't make up a better example of the importance of relationships in behaviour management!

You need to be clear, though, that you aren't in teaching to be the children's friend. You may *become* their friend, but that's different. That's grown out of respect and an appreciation of the asymmetrical power relationship that must exist between you – you are the teacher and they are the student. Start off by establishing clear boundaries and enforcing them. If the homework must be in on Monday or a consequence must follow, a consequence must follow *unless* there is a very good reason why not. Use your common sense, so a claim that the printer ran out of ink may well be made up but *could* be true. Be reasonable and negotiate a new deadline. Of course, if that deadline isn't met the consequence comes into play. You were understanding; you were reasonable; you were *consistent*. Consistency is key here.

If you try to be a tyrant, perfectly reasonable students will resent you; if you make threats but won't carry them through, perfectly reasonable students will try it on. Fair, firm and consistent is what will win over the majority of the class. The students need to know that you are interested in them as individuals (so learn their names as quickly as you can and mark their work to show that you care) and that you will enforce boundaries, but with a sense of perspective.

There are some teachers who never quite grasp the importance of a sense of perspective, but that's important. You want to disrupt the lesson as little as possible so don't rise to every provocation. Eye contact and a shake of the head, a smile, or a finger placed on the lips can be highly effective in stopping trouble before it really happens and yet some teachers feel they have to react in the same way to a student chewing gum and a student killing the boy in the seat next to him. Develop a sense of perspective! If you can, treat it all as a game and rise above it. Of course this is easier said than done with Year 9 on a Friday afternoon, but it's an ideal to work towards.

🔼 brilliant case study

Eddie was forever in trouble both in school and at home. When he was nine he moved from one part of town to another and so had to attend a new primary school. On the first day he met his new headteacher, a very nice man who had seen many examples of emotionally disturbed behaviour. Eddie's first response was to call the headteacher a 'bald headed c***'! Eddie was suspended from school on numerous occasions both at primary and secondary level for a host of misdemeanours. He would take every opportunity to attract attention and would take advantage of any weaknesses he perceived in a teacher. His disruptive behaviour got to such a level that eventually he was permanently excluded in Year 8 and spent the rest of his educational career in a school that dealt with students with emotional and behavioural difficulties. Later on in life, reflecting on his past, Eddie spoke to an audience of newly qualified teachers about dealing with disruptive behaviour. 'Never get wound up,' he told them. 'It was always my intention to wind the teachers up and nine times out of ten I succeeded. Whatever you do, and however you feel, never let a kid know that you are wound up.' Fantastic advice for any teacher.

Of course, all of this is easy to say, harder to do and harder still to do consistently. The idea is to try to do the right thing whenever you can so that the practice starts to make the response second nature. Remember back to when you were starting to learn how to drive (and if you haven't learnt, make up your own analogy!) – remember all the concentration it took to coordinate changing gears and so on. And then one day it occurred to you that you were doing those things unconsciously. The practice meant that they had become second nature. Behaviour management is a bit like that: at first you have to think through how to respond but over time you just start to do it and you don't appreciate how well you are doing because, as far as you are concerned, it just happens.

brilliant tip

Be conscious of your voice and of how you use the space in the classroom. Avoid raising your voice as much as possible, but try to have a really loud bellow for rare, but special, occasions – the shock value is highly effective! There's something about a voice rising in pitch that suggests panic is about to happen so, if you need to compete with a loud class, deliberately *drop* the pitch of your voice – it cuts through the chatter but also seems to convey a sense of authority and calm.

▶

Teachers who aren't feeling confident tend to back themselves up against the board or hide behind their desks – don't! Dominate the space and show that you control the whole room. If the furniture is arranged in such a way that some parts of the room aren't easily accessible, rearrange it, if possible. Send out the clear message that you are in charge of *everywhere* and reinforce this by constantly circulating around the room. With a little practice it is perfectly possible to read aloud from the textbook while moving and scanning what's going on. And if you stumble over a bag, join in the laughter because a teacher nearly falling over in class is genuinely funny!

Basic things to do

The most common behaviour problems are low-level disruption from a few individuals (we'll deal with the awkward class later in the chapter). There are some very straightforward things that you can do that will reduce the amount of disciplining that you have to do later.

Modelling good behaviour in your own room and around the school is essential. Hold doors open for students, say 'please' and 'thank you', be as cheerful as possible with everyone. When you are in the wrong, apologise. Don't be afraid to step away from a confrontation and deal with it later in a low-key way when everyone is calm. If you show that these kinds of things matter, your students are more likely to behave in the way you want.

The importance of knowing students' names and using them can't be emphasised enough. So, greet everyone you pass in the corridors by name, if you can, whether you teach them or whether you don't. Stop students to tell them that you recognise their face but can't put a name to it yet and then make a point of using their name the next time you come across them. Take time to ask students you no longer teach how they are getting on. You are showing that you care about individuals and, also, making sure that students aren't able to feel anonymous in your presence. If you have to break up an unpleasant incident at lunchtime, would you rather try to move on 50 strangers or a bunch of people you can address by name? Of course it's hard to know the names of everyone in a big school but that's not an excuse for not trying!

The importance of learning names connects up with the importance of recognising that different students respond best to different approaches. Management books on getting the best out of others and forming teams can be useful to classroom teachers because managing individuals and classes is what you are doing all the time. Know what works for motivating different individuals because the more motivated they are, the less disruption you will have to deal with.

Use lots of praise but do it when it's merited and do it sincerely. Anyone who has observed lots of lessons will be able to recall teachers whose praise was counter-productive because it was obvious that the students hadn't done anything praiseworthy and knew it! Encouraging students, making them feel they are getting on well and learning something, reduces the likelihood of you having to respond forcefully to poor

use lots of praise

behaviour. If your school has a rewards policy, use it; if the rewards policy doesn't work for an individual or a class, find an alternative way of expressing your appreciation of them. Almost all children appreciate communication with home to say how well they have done.

Try to do interesting things in lessons; swap round the types of activities (bored children and children who have no chance of being successful with a task are much less likely to behave well), differentiate and assess the work so that students know that what they are doing is valued. Be sure to keep scanning the class throughout the lesson.

brilliant tip

Never let your attention stray from what is going on around you. Teachers who have discipline problems usually, in our experience, don't notice what is going on and so are not in a position to nip things in the bud. Deliberately look around you every 10 seconds or so. Make sure that when you are working with an individual or a group you are positioned so that as few students as possible are behind you – and keep scanning what is going on. Never let yourself become engrossed in a conversation, no matter how fascinating it is. We've seen a class playing a game of running out of the classroom, touching the opposite wall of the corridor and running back to their seats *without the teacher noticing*! She was so taken up with the work of her star student that she had forgotten the rest of the class who took advantage of the opportunity. And of course they'll take advantage of the opportunity – they are kids, after all! Make sure that they know that you are watching everything and then they are less likely to try.

All of this will *minimise* the amount of time you have to devote to disciplining students, but still there will be occasions when you have to deal with incidents involving individuals and sometimes you will find yourself with 'the difficult class'.

Be clear about expectations and consequences. Follow up on everything that you've said and make it plain that you mean what you say. Be firm!

Let's take one example – you want the class to listen to instructions. We'll take it for granted that you've thought about how to deliver the instructions and how to help those who struggle to retain information so this is purely about the *behavioural* aspects of the situation. Just about every teacher asks students to stop talking, to stop what they are doing and to look at her/him. Very few teachers then insist on this happening. It's important that you keep reinforcing your expectations.

Try to disrupt the flow of the lesson as little as possible but make sure that everything is dealt with in a low-key manner. Make eye contact with students and shake your head if they have a pen in their hands or put your finger to your lips if they are talking. Drop into the instructions the names of those students whose focus has wavered: 'The next thing we'll do, Laura, is …' This will make Laura look up and either stop what she was doing or give you the chance to make significant eye contact. Knowing the students helps you know how to control the situation. You know that you can take the basketball out of Sam's hand and put it on the floor but that if you do that with Charlotte a row of massive proportions may break out. So don't do it with Charlotte – find another strategy that works with her.

And keep smiling! They aren't wicked (usually), they are just children, so show that you *will* get what you want (the pens on the desks, the basketballs on the floor and so on) but that you don't feel threatened or annoyed. So they didn't put their pens down – you will make sure that they do this because it's what you want, but

keep your sense of perspective

it's no big deal. Keep that balance between getting what you want and not creating unnecessary conflict. Keep your sense of perspective.

The difficult individual slows down learning for her or himself and for others. How you react has a big impact because often the teacher is the major source of disruption in the lesson. Keep everything as low key as possible. Think carefully about who is sitting where to create the most positive combinations of students and to keep students who will spark off each other apart. Try to respond with humour to situations – it reduces the tension – and be happy to laugh at yourself. If the student still isn't doing what's required, then keep on being calm and courteous but point out (preferably to the student, not to the whole class) that the choice is between doing as asked or an appropriate consequence – the student is making the choice. Don't get drawn into rows about what other people are doing; simply say that you'll discuss things at the end of the lesson but for now the student must choose between doing as asked or taking the consequence. Then follow through if s/he makes the wrong choice.

> be happy to laugh at yourself

brilliant example

Let's assume that two boys are talking when they should be doing something else. You point out that either they concentrate on what you want them to do or they will be separated. They continue to chat. You go over, get out a coin and ask one to call, heads or tails? You ask the student who loses to move to a seat of your choice. The student complains that it isn't fair. You tell him you will be happy to discuss this later but for now you want him to move to the other seat. He says he's not going to move. You shrug and smile. If he doesn't move, you explain, you'll have to have him removed from the classroom by a senior teacher. You ask him to move again. He says no. You explain that this is his choice – do as you've asked or be removed with all that that entails – and take your phone and dial up the number that will summon someone to the classroom. Finger poised you ask him if he is sure about what he is choosing. He crashes around a lot, goes to the new place and sulks. You don't rise to all the disruption he tried to cause (you won, after all!) and when he's had a minute or so to calm down you spend a little time with him, thank him for moving, make sure he knows what has to be done and then move on. If he didn't move you must have him removed but later you should speak with him to hear his thoughts and to explain why he had to be taken out.

Keep calm, keep smiling, do just what you say you will, don't take it personally. Maximum effect with minimal disruption is what you are seeking.

Often there will be low-level disruption, no matter what you do, but your intention must be to minimise this. The better you know individuals, the more likely you are to be able to find the right way to work with them. The school's discipline policy should be there to help you but, in the end, no one can do the disciplining for you (and you can't do it for someone else); you use the policy and the support of colleagues to help you create the atmosphere that you want in your class. You can't turn back time and prevent incidents that have occurred already so your intention always should be to reduce the chances of a similar incident occurring in the future. Learn from the experience.

The difficult class

There are some classes that are genuinely challenging, although this is always about the context (your impossible class might look like a doddle to someone in another school). If you've got a genuinely difficult class a good starting point is to break down the mass into the component parts. Take a class list and identify the individuals and the problems. Often it is surprising how many are perfectly good students, but they disappear from view under the awfulness of a comparatively few students who dominate the class. Divide and rule is a good tactic here. Don't, under any circumstances, punish the class. The danger is that a class ethos becomes established and that they find the need to live down to their reputation. You don't want to construct a 'them and us' situation where the class are put into opposition to you – you want 'them and us' to be you and the majority of the class in opposition to the difficult students. 'A few people are spoiling it for the rest of us!' not 'This is the worst class in the school!' Now work at getting individuals on side.

If the class are posing problems for everyone, can one or two key students be moved permanently to another class? Certainly there are combinations of students who bring out the worst in each other, just as some combinations are immediately harmonious. Don't worry about taking extreme measures in the short term for long-term gain. Removing a couple of very difficult students from your lessons for a week or more so that the class can experience how good life is without them can help establish a more positive ethos. A class may be difficult but that class is still made up of many individuals and you can get almost all working with you. Don't be tempted to do only the dullest work possible with them ('I can't trust you so there'll be no more practical work until I can!') because you are only building up more problems for yourself by alienating more and more of the students.

brilliant tip

The benefits of observing cannot be underestimated. Whilst observations can be seen as something to be feared they can also be used as a tool for improvement. If possible, pair up with a colleague and agree to observe each other's lessons. It is even better if you teach the same class as you can share tips. Quite often you will pick up ideas that you would not have thought about otherwise. Yes, it is time-consuming and we can already hear some of you saying, 'Great idea, but where will I get the time?' The answer is to *make* the time. In the long term it can only serve to enhance your practice. With the difficult class, observation is even more important and potentially useful. If you can catch a student being motivated and working hard in someone else's class you are in a position to analyse what it was that had that positive effect and try to replicate it in your lessons.

The impossible individual

There will be some students who will pose you massive problems, no matter what you do. The number of real problem students will vary from school to school but these students need to be worked with. Effective use of teaching assistants can help minimise disruption for other students, but you need to accept the reality that you will have students in your lessons who cannot (note: cannot, not will not!) behave to the standard that the others can. Know as much as you can about these students and then try to square the circle of giving them the best education you can while not disrupting the education of the majority of the class. The most useful advice about dealing with those 'impossible' students can only be learned from people who know that child and your school. By definition, these are the children where generalisations just don't apply. We're sorry if this sounds like a cop-out but the best advice here really is to listen to your local expert.

 brilliant recap

- Getting the discipline right is essential to making learning happen.
- Keep calm under all provocation and don't take things personally.
- Know the individuals who make up a class and develop a sense of which strategies work best for each individual.
- Have expectations you can enforce and follow through on consequences.
- Have a sense of humour and a sense of proportion.
- Be reasonable and understanding.
- Move around the room, scanning all of the time, to prevent incidents before they occur.

▶

- Disrupt lessons as little as possible – try to deal with incidents quietly.
- Remember that most children want to learn but they will challenge you to find out the boundaries, so make the boundaries clear.
- Use the school discipline and support structures.
- Never punish a class for the misdemeanours of a few.

Summary

Behaviour management is something that almost all teachers get better at without ever quite noticing that it's happening and many have a lower opinion of their abilities than is really justified. Patience, calmness, a sense of humour and consistency will solve the vast majority of your problems but engaging lessons and making it clear that you truly care about your students will prevent many of those problems in the first place.

Never forget, though, that the classroom is a complicated place, filled with webs of relationships, and that it is unrealistic to imagine that you will ever get to the point where you never encounter difficulties – too much is happening that is beyond your control. A sensible and realistic approach to problems and a willingness to seek help and advice when necessary will get you a long way.

CHAPTER 5

Up to the mark: formative assessment

I didn't fail the test, I just found 100 ways to get it wrong!

Benjamin Franklin

This chapter isn't about national tests and exams – there's already enough of an obsession about them. It's about the need to keep a grasp of the reality that exams are supposed to be a measure of learning rather than an end in themselves, validating the standard reached rather than being the purpose of education. Our belief is that if you get the teaching and learning right, the results will follow.

This chapter also covers the interventions where teachers try to make a difference to students' learning. Brilliant teachers are assessing all of the time. Marking, asking questions, setting up self- and peer-assessment – constantly students' learning is being assessed and students are being challenged to deepen their thinking. Good *formative* assessment is about deliberately doing things to make sure the student knows what could be improved and how that improvement could be made, thereby ensuring that all students are progressing.

> brilliant teachers are assessing all of the time

Assessment for learning

It was in March 1998 that the journal *Assessment in Education* published an article by Paul Black and Dylan Wiliam that has had a significant impact on the way that teachers assess students' work. In 68 pages they reviewed the published literature on formative assessment (assessment that isn't concerned with grading students' achievements but on assessing work to see how the student could improve her or his performance) and used this to suggest how teachers could bring about a real improvement in student achievement. This led to a shorter, more accessible pamphlet – *Inside the Black Box* – and on to a series of pamphlets dealing with assessment for learning (as it came to be known) in different subjects, a book (*Assessment for Learning*) and a government initiative that ignored some of the key findings and managed to reduce an exciting approach into a series of fairly mechanical processes.

If all you know about assessment for learning is the government initiative, you should read *Inside the Black Box*. Urgently!

There's a large and rapidly growing body of literature on assessment for learning and formative assessment. In this chapter all we can do is try to give suggestions as to some of the things you might want to try to do. It's about the way in which you approach teaching, not about traffic-lighting until you and the class are sick of the process; teachers who take formative assessment seriously are in danger of finding it transforms their practice for the better and for ever.

To simplify things enormously, classroom teachers can have a massive impact on achievement by:

- getting students actively involved in the assessment of their own work and the work of others;
- using the information gained from assessments to change what they teach and the way in which they teach it;
- offering advice on how to improve when responding to work and not grading or giving numerical marks.

Marking

Teachers mark work for a whole variety of reasons (because they feel they ought to, in order to keep parents and school management happy and so on) but they tend to lose sight of the primary purpose, which surely is to help the students improve. And if a task doesn't give you the kind of assessment data that allows you to decide how well a student is learning, why did you bother getting students to do it in the first place?

So, the starting point for assessment is setting quality tasks. Don't worry about 'busy work' that will keep the class occupied but not much else – keep asking yourself, 'What will the students gain from this task?' and 'What will I learn about them from it?' We all have days (often at the end of the week or the end of the term) when simply keeping a class busy seems good enough, but don't let it become a habit.

Marking is a time-consuming process. Most teachers don't get enthusiastic about sitting down to a pile of exercise books or worksheets – it's a dull task best done quickly. Think of all that time you've spent marking – what improvement has it produced? Can you honestly say that the learning it produced in your students justified the time and effort that you invested in it? You need to think about how you can get more improvement for no more (or even less) effort.

Everyone can learn – that has to be the starting point for teachers. In the past we've heard teachers asserting that they have classes who will never be able to improve on their current performance, but thankfully we've not heard this for a while now. The thing that must be emphasised is *effort* not native ability. Of course some of us start off with advantages in life, but it's what we do to maximise our potential that's crucial. It'll take students less time or longer to achieve milestones but eventually they can get there. Formative assessment is about helping everyone to make progress at the fastest rate they can. It's not doing a task well that's important, it's a student doing it well compared to their previous performance.

It is at this point that we want to draw your attention to an important issue – not using marks or grades. These encourage students to compare their results and establish a rank order in the class. The consequences almost always will be negative: complacency or demoralisation. Students whose work is responded to with comments on what went well and how it could be improved make much better progress than those whose work is merely graded. Interestingly, if there are marks *and* comments students make no more progress than if there had been marks only and yet many schools are insisting on marks and comments in their marking policies, increasing teachers' workload without increasing the effectiveness of the feedback.

brilliant example

Miss Lively wants to check that students know factual material about a topic but doesn't want to set a test that produces a mark out of 20; she wants the test to help students see where their knowledge is lacking so that they can target their attention on the weak spots. She sets a straightforward recall test that concentrates on the key facts she wants them to know and asks students to do as much as they can in test conditions without referring to friends or to notes and textbooks. They then have time to check their answers and to ask if they are unsure about anything (she targets her help particularly to those who are least likely to have good recall and may even give out a copy of the answers, if it seems appropriate). She quickly runs over the answers and makes sure that she clears up any confusions that seem general. The class are told that next lesson they will have exactly the same questions but in a different order – the expectation is that everyone will get everything right. The focus has shifted from a potentially competitive situation to one where the emphasis is on knowing the material.

At its most basic, you need to ask yourself if the students can read your comments. Some of us are blessed with immaculate handwriting but most of us tend to scrawl, especially when we have been marking for a long time. Ask some of your students to read back to you what you have written. If any of them can't, think of how many hours of your life you could be wasting writing comments that are of no use at all. Similarly, many comments aren't easily understood by the students who are supposed to read them because the language is too complex or the expression too imprecise and careless. It's not enough for you to know what you meant and, again, asking students to explain back to you what they think you meant can be a chastening experience.

Try to keep your comments brief and focused on the strengths of a piece and on one or two things that would make it better. Teachers often imagine that comment-only marking means they must write pages but, of course, most students don't read it all. Cultivate being precise and succinct: focus on the essentials and don't waffle!

> focus on the essentials and don't waffle!

brilliant tip

Consider the possibility of typing some of your comments on to sticky labels and then attaching them to the work. It means the comments are legible, it restricts how much you say (you have to focus on one or two essentials) and you can save a copy on the computer to use at parents' evenings, academic reviews or report-writing time.

Comment-only marking takes time and effort on your part but it repays the effort both in student progress and in personal satisfaction. Ticking and crossing may not take long – we once saw a supply teacher marking a set of books by ticking randomly whilst turning the pages from back to front of an exercise book and at one point he wasn't even looking at the book as he ticked – but it's hard to see it as anything other than a chore. Some people new to this kind of approach set too much written work and try to write too much on every piece; this will lead to exhaustion for you, the marking will pile up and you won't be able to face the backlog.

Set fewer written tasks and approach the marking of those you do set more flexibly. Occasionally you can hear people boasting about how their class have already filled an exercise book and it's only just October, but this is confusing quantity of writing with quality of learning and they aren't the same thing. When you do get the class to write you don't need to mark every piece in the same way and with the same degree of attention to detail. Marking simply can be to acknowledge that you have seen a piece or it can register a basic response ('Yes – you've got it!' or 'I enjoyed this'). This kind of marking works well when you are concerned with students' factual knowledge or when you are responding to a final version of a piece of work. Only mark certain pieces in detail, or mark only some students' work in detail on a rota basis. When you do mark in detail, though, get the maximum benefit from it by, say, marking a draft in some detail but simply acknowledging the final version. You must pace yourself over the year and cultivate a sense of what is possible, and setting two pieces of written work for every student every week and then responding in depth to all of the writing just isn't possible if you want to keep your health!

 **brilliant** timesaver

Before you set a task, think about the assessment and be very clear about what would make a piece successful. What do you want students to be learning and can you isolate just one or two things to comment on? And don't be clear just in your own mind about what the success criteria are; make sure the students know what will make a successful attempt on a task. Try to restrict yourself when you are marking, too: don't start commenting on all kinds of things that weren't part of the original success criteria – keep focused on them!

Don't assume that more writing means more learning. Deliberately find ways of teaching that don't require massive amounts of written product. Keep going back to the basics: what do you want students to learn and what will be the most efficient way of learning that? Look for approaches that won't keep you marking 'busy work' so you've more time to spend on more intensive responses to selected pieces.

One way to improve the impact your marking has is to give students time to respond to your feedback. When you give work back, allow some lesson time for students to read it. Ask them to respond in some way, by making some specific changes to what they have done, by asking them to answer an additional question, or by asking them to explain something about the work to another student. If you don't give time for students to read and act on your feedback the chances are that many (probably most) will not read it. It always strikes us as strange that teachers will invest time in marking books and then begrudge another five minutes in class to actually get the most out of the marking.

Now, test yourself to make sure that you are giving the kind of written feedback that will help the students improve in your subject. Take the exercise books or folders of a couple of students you teach (you need to have several pieces of work that you've responded to if this is going to work). Type up the comments that you have made and then consider how subject-specific they were. The results can be frightening: it isn't unusual to find that there is nothing subject-specific on any piece of work. The bland ('Good work', 'Keep this standard up', 'Not your best work') will rub shoulders with a concern for a proper work ethic ('Use a ruler!', 'You need to concentrate more') but an outsider reading the comments might have no idea which subject was being taught. Now you've frightened yourself, deliberately try to focus on only making comments that will help the student make progress in your subject. Your comment alone should be enough to tell someone what the subject is!

Targets

Targets can make a real difference to how students progress but once again many schools, departments and individual teachers are paying lip service to this. A good basic rule to hold on to is 'If a target doesn't suggest *how* improvement can be made, it's not likely to have an effect.' Frequently teachers add targets (they know they

> targets can make a real difference

should and that they'll be in trouble if they don't!), but no consideration has been given to whether or not the target will produce the desired effect. Bland and anodyne targets are a waste of everyone's time – better to have nothing than the pious hope of 'You must put in more effort' or 'Learn the vocabulary more thoroughly'. These are just another way of telling the student to 'Be better' – they may need guidance that is rather more specific if that is going to happen!

The best targets are the ones that students set for themselves, but if teachers struggle to find something adequate to say, what chance has the student? They will tend to focus on surface features of their work (spelling, handwriting, etc.) or on work ethic. Students need training in target setting and teachers must persist with it. Often we are too concerned with imparting content to worry about whether or not it is being learned, but teachers must give time over to helping students learn how to evaluate their own successes and set their own targets for improvement.

Yes, at first students will suggest targets like working harder or being better at spelling but, with a bit of time and effort, they can be helped to frame more helpful targets that are more specific and achievable.

Setting targets doesn't have to be formal; it doesn't have to have a special ritual or formula attached to it. At its most basic it is simply asking a student to think about what would make their work better and what they could do to bring about that improvement.

Learning objectives

Writing learning objectives on the board started off as something that teachers did in order to help students focus on what the point of the lesson was, because, as most of us will have noticed, what we think we are teaching and what the students think they are learning often are not the same thing at all. Over time, though, it has become the expectation that teachers will share learning objectives and this means that more often than not this is just lip service – teachers write up learning objectives not to help students but because they feel they have to in order to make the school leadership or inspectors happy. These objectives are often a statement of the content of the lesson and are phrased in such a way that only another teacher could decipher what is meant with no attempt to explain things to students in language that they will understand.

Learning objectives should be understood by the students and that means thinking about the language you use. There should be only one or two learning objectives. The learning objectives need to be talked through. Presenting the class with the objectives, telling them to copy them down and then starting the lesson with no more explanation is doing no one any good.

brilliant dos and don'ts

Do

✔ Make sure the learning objectives are phrased in language students will understand.

✔ Make sure the learning objectives are not just a statement of what the task is.

✔ Make it clear why you think this learning is worthwhile and how it fits into the bigger picture of the unit of work.

✔ Explain what a good piece of work will look like so students know what they are aiming for.

Don't

✘ Have too many learning objectives – keep it simple.

✘ Forget the learning objectives altogether.

✘ Be too slavishly tied to the learning objectives – be prepared to be taken into new places if it seems appropriate.

We've spoken about plenaries in Chapter 3 because you need to have planned them in order to get maximum benefit out of them, but they need to be mentioned again here because, at their best, they allow teachers to judge to what extent learning has happened. A colleague once explained that he had tested a class and that the test showed that almost no one had a clear grasp of what he had just taught them. So what did he do? He moved on to the next topic because he had to cover the specification. 'Covering the specification' has, for many teachers, become more important than ensuring that students learn. A plenary is a device that lets you know whether it is right to move on to whatever you had planned next or whether a rethink is in order. You may feel that you taught it to them and they *should* have learned it, but if they have got the wrong end of the stick the plenary should give you the chance to find that out and do something about it.

Questioning

One book that has had a big impact on many of its readers is *Invisible Children* by James Pye. In it he talks about those students who we taught but can't remember – the ones who faded into the background and rendered themselves invisible. Pye suggests that these students inhabit *Nomansland* and are trying, for a variety of reasons, to avoid activity and attention. It's a book about wasted potential and about the teacher's responsibility to draw out those students, to make them participate and make the most of their chances in school. Skilful questioning will definitely help you get *all* students more involved in lessons.

Teachers wait a ridiculously short time before expecting classes to answer their questions, but just because we know the answer doesn't mean that it is on the tip of all the students' tongues! Taking answers only from students with their hands up will effectively shut out most of the class from any direct involvement, so create situations where everyone can be expected to provide an answer. Thinking time can be a useful strategy here: 'I'm going to ask you a question in a moment and I want you to think about what you think the answer is for 20 seconds, then I'm going to pick on two or three people to suggest an answer.' But even more useful is getting pairs or fours to talk about the question so that everyone is forced to consider it.

Of course, this has implications for the type of questions that you ask. If all your questions are simply factual recall it's probable that many students won't be able to answer, no matter how long you wait. You need to be asking richer, open questions. You also need to work at asking follow-up questions that make students explain their thinking. Make students respond to each other's answers, justifying or criticising the response. Some useful prompts to encourage deeper thinking might be:

make students respond to each other's answers

- X, what do you think about Y's answer? Does it convince you?
- Explain to us *why* you think that is the answer.
- Would that answer be right in all situations?
- Has anyone any other suggestions? (Useful especially if the first answer was a really good one!)
- Talk to the person next to you for one minute and identify at least one thing about Y's answer that could be improved on.
- That's interesting but what if …?
- Was she right? Why? Why not?
- Are you sure?

And, of course, these questions could be discussed profitably in small groups before you take an answer.

You want to be gathering information not just about *what* students know but also about *how* they arrived at their answers. Be less concerned with the facts they know and more with the thought processes that are going on. If they have a misconception, why do they have it? Your role at this point isn't to tell them whether they are right or wrong but to help them understand things more fully and to help correct misunderstandings. The wrong answer for the right reason or the right answer for the wrong reason can be really handy as ways to explore the key question: do they understand?

The mood in the classroom has to be right if you are going to encourage this kind of exploratory thinking – students need to know that being wrong is okay and that wrong answers are often the starting point for learning. This has to be cultivated over time, but when you get to the point when it is no big deal to say, 'Reuben hasn't quite got that right – can you see what the mistake is?' then learning can *really* happen!

From the very start of the year don't ask the students to put up their hands to volunteer answers; insist on a no hands-up rule.

Everyone must be able to attempt an answer to all questions. Because you allow thinking time and discussion, and have a secure classroom where learning from mistakes is seen as positive, everyone will be able to have a go.

brilliant tip

If any students claim not to have an answer, tell them you'll be back to them after you've taken another answer. If they still won't or can't answer, catch them on their own and explain that they will be the first responder to the next question and, if necessary, give them extra advance notice of what the question will be. Don't let them off the hook, though – no one must be allowed to opt out of thinking! If they are looking for a quiet life, keep on at them; if they are slow processors of information, give them the additional warning and help so that they can participate.

It can be useful to get students to come up with their own questions that they genuinely want to know the answer to and then to get other students to answer them. (It's a handy plenary technique, too.) Often you will find that the students want to know things that seem self-evident to you ('What does this word mean?') and, of course, you will need to work with them, over a matter of months, helping them frame ever more demanding questions. Time spent like that is an investment, not a waste. Of course *teachers* all know what 'persiflage' means – doesn't everyone? – and they can solve Fermat's theorem at the drop of a hat; remember that, in your class, the student with the confidence and skills to articulate the question most of the class need to know the answer to is the student who is in control of their own learning.

Self- and peer-assessment

As with so much else, students need training if they are to be able to look critically and evaluatively at their own work and at the work of their peers. Many (probably most) students find self-assessment really hard. If they had known what they should have done better they would have done it better first time! Breaking the class in gently with lots of peer-assessment is often a good idea – it's easier to spot the strong and weak points in someone else's work than it is in your own.

It's always a good idea to give students a really clear framework when they are assessing work, whether it's written or oral. Make sure that they know what 'good' looks like and guide them away from over-concentration on surface features such as hand-writing, neatness, spelling and so on. Modelling the process for the class is a really effective way of helping them appreciate what it is they are looking for. Over time you can step back more and more, getting them to 'mark' their own work before handing it in so that your job is to validate their own judgements. Some will take longer than others to grasp how to do this and this means that you will need to offer more support to some than to others. Your job is to make yourself redundant as the person who decides what is good and what isn't, freeing you to suggest how students can make the improvements they have identified as necessary. Producing independent learners is the aim.

> producing independent learners is the aim

Peer-assessment relies, as so much else does, on the relationships within the class. There are opportunities here for students to make each other very unhappy and the teacher needs to manage groupings, teach tact and, above all, create the belief that mistakes aid learning.

brilliant example

Mr Whitaker wants his Year 8 class to do presentations to the class, but he knows that these are often very badly done. This year he spends part of a lesson making sure the class know what a good presentation looks like – simple things such as looking at the audience, speaking loudly, not reading a script, not picking your nose when someone else in the group is doing the talking. As the groups prepare he asks a fairly confident bunch if they will do their presentation early for the rest of the class to see and assess. They agree because the atmosphere in the classroom is such that risk-taking is okay.

On the day of the presentation Mr Whitaker gives the rest of the class specific things to look out for. Some are to focus on the presenters' body language, some on clarity of explanation and so on. At the end of the presentation there is an extensive deconstruction of what has gone on. Students have been told to concentrate on what was good, but carefully chosen tactful students have been given the task of identifying one significant weakness in each presenter (the teacher knows the group dynamics so there's no chance of him letting kids who don't get on having an opportunity to settle scores in public). Mr Whitaker is an active participant in all this, validating judgements or offering modifications if he thinks someone is being too critical or too generous. He knows the class and how much public honesty each individual can stand!

Now everyone knows what makes for a good presentation and they've looked at the presentation with a critical eye. They get some more time to polish up what they are going to do and the group who've done the trial run have some specifics to work on – targets, in effect.

When the presentations take place Mr Whitaker gives every individual a sheet on which to record impressions. The sheets require a comment on both subject content and presentation skills, and has prompts on it – the kinds of things that the class commented on during the trial-run. Each member of the audience has one presenter to focus on for their comments and knows that the balance of positive features (with examples) to areas for improvement should be three to one.

▶

Each group's presentation is followed by brief feedback from the class (Mr Whitaker warns those who will be asked to comment *before* the presentation starts and then allows three or four volunteers who feel they have something significant to add). At the end Mr Whitaker takes in the comment sheets, checks them to make sure there is nothing offensive or malicious on them (he may be idealistic but he's no mug either!) and copies them. He passes the originals on to the relevant presenter so each student gets notes on their performance from four or five other students. They then write a paragraph or two about the experience, what went well and what they will improve on next time.

All of this gets revisited when they do another presentation, but now the focus is on making at least one significant improvement to technique: 'This time I'm going to make more eye contact with the audience. I'll do this by scanning the room all the time and I've asked Liz to put her hand up if she notices that I've stopped doing this.'

Mr Whitaker emails his colleagues who teach the class to tell them about the notes he's got on their presentational skills in case they want to use them (thereby doing his bit to disseminate good practice) and, at the end of the year, passes everything on to their next teacher who can now build on their skills.

There is constant peer- and self-assessment going on, everyone is learning and Mr Whitaker knows it!

Pulling it all together

Over the years we've used a variety of techniques that encourage students to get more involved in thinking about how much they are learning. The following is a fairly random list of them but we are confident that they are useful additions to a teacher's repertoire of approaches. Some we've discussed in more detail in this chapter but for some we've added a brief explanation of what's involved.

- Traffic-lighting (students judge how confident they are about their knowledge or skills by indicating if they are 'green' (confident), 'amber' (some doubts) or 'red' (very unsure). A good way forward here is to get the greens to explain things to the ambers (and to ask you for help if necessary) while you work with the reds.

- Time to think/waiting time when a question is asked.
- Time to discuss a whole-class question with a partner.
- Advance warning of questions.
- No hands up (everyone must be able to offer an answer – use the three previous techniques to get everyone to the point where they can answer).
- Follow-up questions ('Why was that right?').
- Open-ended provocative questions thrown in after listening to a group discussing (and not waiting for the answer).
- Student self- and peer-assessment (oral and written work).
- Exemplars (making available good examples of work or answers to questions and then discussing what made them so good).
- Modelling (going through a process such as writing the conclusion to an essay in real time in front of the class, talking about what it is you are doing).
- Marking/doing tests with a partner and textbook/notes.

 brilliant recap

- Avoid marks and grades in favour of comments as much as your school will allow you to – focus on what is going well and how work could be improved (and, crucially, *how*).
- Don't mark all work in equal depth. Target your effort to where it will produce maximum effect and provide response time for students when you return marked work.

▶

- Make sure you communicate clearly with students, especially when writing.

- Skilful questioning increases student involvement in lessons and helps you see if students really understand.

Summary

Keep reminding yourself that the process and the methods of assessment are not the purpose but the means to achieving the purpose: learning. You want the students to be better in your subject and things like writing up learning objectives, setting specific, measurable, agreed, realistic and time-based (SMART) targets, 'traffic-lighting' and so on may well help them achieve that goal. Those methods aren't an end in themselves, though. Don't fall into the trap of doing things because that's what you do; do things because you can see that they make a difference. And if they don't make a difference, do something else!

CHAPTER 6

The data day business: using data for pupil improvement

(When analysing data) you should stop when you've reached simplicity.

Henri Poincaré

L ots of teachers are frightened by data, but they shouldn't be. Data isn't there to make life complicated – it's the *attitude* towards data that's the potential enemy, not the data itself; data is neutral stuff.

So, what is data?

A dictionary definition probably will be along the lines of it being known facts that allow you to draw inferences from them (also it will probably tell you that *data* is a plural noun, but we'll be using it as a singular). Of course this sounds nicely scientific. No one could ever object to facts, could they? And facts will tell us the truth.

Don't be fooled – most of the quantitative data that is used in schools is treated as if it were a great deal more certain and reliable than it really is, and the brilliant classroom teacher needs to be able to treat it with a healthy scepticism, though not with unhealthy cynicism. It's the inferences that you draw from the data that will help you teach more effectively, not the mere existence of the data in a markbook or on a spreadsheet.

Quantitative or qualitative?

Let's simplify things and assume that there are two types of data in school: quantitative and qualitative. Both have their place and both need to be treated differently.

Data is used mostly in school nowadays to mean *quantitative* information that you've got about students and classes that you teach – numbers, grades, levels and so on that will allow you to arrange students in some kind of hierarchy. Some of this data you'll be given (Fischer Family Trust estimates, for example, or standardised test scores) and some of it you'll generate yourself (test results, 'levels' given to pieces of work and so on).

We'd like you to give consideration to *qualitative* data, too. What the primary school said in a Year 6 report is data. What other teachers say about students' ability and potential in reports is data. What *you* observe about the students is data. Numbers generated by a computer look authoritative but you have your own observations to contribute – you appreciate and understand things in a way that numbers alone will never be able to represent. Don't undervalue your skill and experience, or the skill and experience of your colleagues.

> don't undervalue your skill and experience

We've gone for a very rough and ready definition of data because it has the advantage of being inexact. Too many teachers react to quantitative data as if it were infallible truth, even if it contradicts what they observe every day in the classroom. Quantitative data *won't* answer questions – you have to do that – but it *will* help suggest the interesting questions you should be asking. It won't tell you *how* to teach something but it might help you to see what needs to be taught differently. Don't analyse data to death – use it to help you focus in so that you can see something that needs improving and then plan how to bring about the improvement. The end product isn't the data or the analysis but improved teaching and learning. Stop when you reach simplicity!

Qualitative data

If quantitative data tends to be treated with too much reverence, qualitative data is very much the Cinderella these days.

There are a mass of useful words about students in school filing cabinets but, because they aren't so easily pulled together as numbers can be, they get underused.

brilliant tip

Do an audit of the qualitative data that is available to you about your students. In written form there will be records from primary school, reports, records of meetings with parents and so on. There will also be anecdotal material; colleagues will have a story to tell about the day that James was motivated by something, or some approach that they used to teach him something that really worked. Know where to find the data that might help you do a better job with a student. All the words and stories about students (treated with sufficient scepticism and weighed against your own experience) are a resource you need to be able to access and use.

We're going to pass over the data that already exists (once you've got in mind what there is you can locate it as and when necessary) and focus more on collecting your own qualitative data. In particular we want to recommend the use of interviews and questionnaires to make you an even better teacher.

Interviews

If you want to know what people think, the easiest way probably is to ask them. Often we make assumptions about our students and base our decisions on them, but with a little time and effort we can discover all sorts of things that will help us in our teaching. Which lessons did the class actually enjoy and why? Under what kind of conditions do they learn best? How do they feel about homework? When we start to find out the answers to some of these questions we can start to adjust what we do to make it more effective.

Of course it would be possible to pick up information from casual chats, but a slightly more formal situation with an interview schedule makes sure that you cover the points that you want to rather than getting hopelessly distracted. Think through which questions to ask, how to phrase them and how to order them before you start. Try to avoid leading questions. Aim for the session to last about 30 minutes or less and know which of your questions are essential and which you could cut if time gets short. You want to try to focus on something fairly specific that you want to find out rather than just have a random list of questions. How do students feel they learn best in this subject? What do students feel about the homeworks they are set? Plan your questions to address your central concern and leave the questions open-ended. Having eight to ten questions will be enough, but be sure that you really listen to the answers and follow up points that students make – all those types of question that you might ask in class to deepen understanding will be useful here, too.

Try to have the interview in a room where you won't be disturbed and make sure you are all sitting where you can make eye contact with each other. Don't segregate yourself behind a desk and don't spend so much time writing that you never get to look at the speaker and encourage them. It's always possible to record the interview and transcribe it later, but this does create a rather more unnatural atmosphere and there never does seem to be the time to play the tape back! The more awkward the mood and physically uncomfortable the space, the lower the quality of your data is likely to be – try to put everyone at their ease.

> try to put everyone at their ease

Experience suggests that three is an ideal number of students to interview at one time and that single-sex groups tend to produce fewer arguments. It also allows you to explore gender variations.

It is easy to choose only the students you want to ask but it is important to get a genuine cross-section of the class – if Demi is a grumpy little so-and-so who never smiles and never enjoys anything you do, then the temptation is to avoid her but she is exactly the kind of student you most need to engage. Randomising the way you pick students is sensible (within the constraint of keeping a single-sex group); over time you will cover a cross-section of students. If you don't randomly select who you will speak to, unintentional bias is sure to creep in.

brilliant tip

If you want to randomise things then a dice (another plural noun we're using as a singular!) is a helpful tool and a 30-sided dice is particularly useful. These are found easily in games shops, especially those that cater for fantasy role-playing games. Get your class list, roll the dice and select the student who is that number on your register. If they are the wrong sex for the group you are constructing take the next student going down the list who is the right sex (and if you fall off the bottom of the list, start again at the top). You can use the dice in class, too, to pick who is going to speak first, answer the next question and so on.

During the interview be friendly but do all that you can to avoid leading the students. Try not to give the impression that there are some answers that you want to hear because you may find that students are being less than honest and are trying to second-guess you. Studied neutrality is the best pose to adopt.

Once you've collected your data you need to do something with it. Think about what the implications might be and discuss these with colleagues. If the students say something that just doesn't sound right, think about why this is. If everything that gets said confirms your beliefs, think back and make sure that you weren't leading them. Now draw up plans for modifying what you do to take account of what you've learned.

---

brilliant example

Here's a possible schedule that you could use with Year 7 or 8 students to try to find out a bit more about their attitudes towards your subject (subject X). There's nothing terribly clever about this but it has the virtue of using very open questions and of not leading students too much. The simplicity is the virtue.

- What is your favourite subject in school? Why?
- What do you most like about subject X?
- What do you like least?
- Describe a good lesson that we've had in subject X – what made it so good?
- Describe a bad lesson that we've had in subject X – what made it so bad?
- Do you think you are making good progress in subject X? How do you know this?
- What do you think you need to do to improve in subject X?
- If you could change two things about the lessons in subject X, what would they be? Why?

Questionnaires

Questionnaires are useful for collecting information about individuals' attitudes and behaviour (in which case you want names on them). They are also useful for collecting very broad impressions from a largish number of people (a whole class, say) in which case you might want to keep the results anonymous, but get the respondent to indicate their sex or any other variable you think might be significant for these particular questions. The hard work comes in constructing the right questions, putting them in the right order and then trying to make sense of the responses. Simple questionnaires that require respondents to indicate an answer from a list ('How long do you usually spend on homework in an average week? (a) less than one hour; (b) between one and three hours; (c) between three and five hours; (d) more than five hours) are easy to analyse. How many of each response did you get? Questionnaires that require the respondent to create their own answer ('What do you think are the reasons we have homework?') are much harder to analyse because you need to try to find ways to group answers together and deciding on the boundaries between categories can be tricky, but they will raise interesting issues that you might choose to probe more deeply in interviews.

 **brilliant** timesaver

Before creating a questionnaire stop and think about exactly what you want to find out. It's not uncommon for people to put together a mish-mash of questions and then, after looking at the results, realise that they are no wiser about the key topic than they were when they started. A little time planning and testing the questionnaire on a couple of people will prevent you from wasting hours trying to analyse responses to ambiguous or irrelevant questions.

Remember that you are not getting certainties with the responses but perceptions. If you ask students whether they get too much, just enough or too little group work in class, their responses don't tell you whether you are getting the amount right or not – they tell you what the students feel and that's not the same thing. If your students tell you they feel there should be more group work, don't immediately build in lots more but think back to how much actually has happened. Are you happy with the amount? Follow up by conducting a structured interview with some students to see why they feel as they do. The questionnaire suggests what needs to be considered in more depth.

Quantitative data

Perhaps the key thing to keep in mind about quantitative data is that it must be treated with a healthy degree of scepticism. Don't claim that the data *proves* anything, the data will *suggest* and then it is up to you to discover if that suggestion is valid or if there are alternative explanations that are equally or more valid.

Let's practise being sceptical by looking at one aspect of many commercial tests, the way results are given as a standard age score (SAS). This is produced by taking the raw score (the mark that the student got) and the age of the student on the day when the test was taken. There will be a look-up table in the test manual that enables the raw score that a student got (the actual mark they got) to be converted into a SAS. Say two students get a raw score of 40 on a test but, on the date on which they took it, one was only just 11 and the other was nearly 12. The younger student will get a higher SAS than the older. The SAS tells you how a student is performing when compared to the average performance for her or his age. The average performance score is represented as a SAS of 100.

This looks very exciting when you see a whole class or, better still, a whole year group in SAS order. Now you know exactly who is the cleverest and who is the least clever, surely? You've got a definitive rank order, haven't you? Well, no. It looks like you do, but this is overlooking *the margin of error*. All commercially produced tests that produce a quantitative score will tell you about the margin of error. It stands to reason that you can't measure things as vague as 'cognitive ability' or 'spelling ability' with absolute precision.

The publishers of tests will tell you what the confidence band is for a test or for part of a test. This is because test results are influenced by a whole range of factors. A student may be feeling ill or particularly nervous on the day of a test, for example. If they retook the test the next day they might get some questions wrong that they got right today (or vice versa). Schools and teachers often (*usually* is probably more true) treat test results as being a lot more accurate than the test publishers' claims would justify. And how much more true is this of teacher-created tests?

The danger is that you will treat the complicated data that standard age scores represent in an over-simplified way. You might rank order the students and draw a line across the list – those who score 117 on a test get on to the gifted and talented programme; those who score 'only' 116 don't make it! Using confidence bands means that you appreciate that the reality is a great deal less black and white than the initial impression. If you retested the students, the rank order wouldn't come out the same.

Another source of data that is often over-simplified is the information that comes from the Fischer Family Trust (FFT). The Fischer Family Trust is a charitable organisation that produces data to help schools in the process of analysis and target setting. All too often, though, FFT data is seen as the bane of the classroom teacher's life.

The best indicator of future performance is past performance. FFT is based on how students performed in the past and extrapolates from that by telling you how other students with similar performances at KS2, KS3 or GCSE went on to perform, *on average*, in the future. It doesn't give a guarantee that this is how students will perform; it gives an indication of how students have, *on average*, performed and uses this to suggest future possibilities. It gives an estimate and not a prediction. If a racehorse has been last in his previous four outings then

> the best indicator of future performance is past performance

the chances are he won't win his next race. He *might*, but it's not likely and the bookmakers' odds will reflect this improbability. If a student did poorly at KS2 he *might* do exceptionally well at KS3 but it's not very likely and the FFT estimate will reflect this improbability.

Most commercial tests, like the widely used Cognitive Abilities Test, are not based on prior attainment but on a more abstract concept (in this case, cognitive ability). A student may score very highly on CATs but may not have been very successful in school or they may have a low CAT score but be comparatively successful in school. A good attitude, supportive parents and brilliant teachers can have had a positive effect on actual achievement. Because the data looks imposing, though, and is often presented as if it is giving absolute truths, many teachers accept it at face value. Be wary of casting students with low scores or low estimates as being condemned to failure – the brilliant teacher needs to be reading the data with more subtlety. You and they may have to work that bit harder but they can always outperform the estimates.

Teachers don't need more data about students and classes; they need to put the data that they have got to better use. What you want to do is to make the data work for you, to make it help you teach your students more effectively. Data is most useful when it is making you ask questions, so look at the data you hold on some of the students you teach.

---

brilliant example

Fischer Family Trust (FFT) data is often disparaged by classroom teachers. Many classroom teachers feel that they are being saddled with unrealistic expectations (schools and teachers treat the estimates as predictions) and this can lead to cynicism ('I'd like to see them get Becky an A!'). Instead, ask yourself why Becky isn't performing at the FFT estimate.

Maybe Becky has acquired an extreme interest in what we will politely call 'recreational activities'. Maybe her family are going through a really rough patch. For most Beckys, though, you could come up with some reasons for underachievement that you might be able to do something about. It might be something very specific to Becky in your subject (she lacks a skill or finds a particular group of concepts difficult); it might be a general approach to learning (she doesn't put herself out to learn); it might be as basic as poor attendance (if she isn't in class she isn't going to learn what was taught).

Okay, now talk to Becky about this.

'There's a problem: the data says that you've got the potential to get an A at GCSE but you aren't going to on current performance. What do *you* think is going wrong? What can *we* do to improve your performance?'

Show Becky the data (students are suitably impressed by authoritative-looking data, just like teachers are). Listen to what she says – really listen, don't just let her speak and then say what you have planned. Be honest with her – if she is deluding herself, tell her. Help her to articulate what needs to be done. Help her plan out how to improve. Help her check to see if she is on track. The data has allowed you to have a conversation that gives Becky the chance to achieve more highly. You can't make her be successful but you can help her to see how she can achieve more.

There's a book that's been around for many years now, *Pygmalion in the Classroom* by Rosenthal and Jacobson. The subtitle of the book, *Teacher expectations and pupils' intellectual development*, says it all. Look at the data you've got with the expectation that it will raise your expectations and the expectations of the student. If one estimate is higher than the others, believe the highest and make the student believe it too. Then use this as a way to talk about how they can achieve more highly. The data is the lever that you use in order to raise the student's aspirations. What the data *is* actually doesn't matter that much, from this point of view; what's important is the way that you use it. In *Pygmalion in the Classroom* the data that led to student progress was made up but it changed the perceptions of teachers and students and led to genuine improvements in performance.

↗ brilliant case study

Sara came into secondary school with lowish KS2 results and ended up in set 3 of 4 in maths. However, her teacher spotted an anomaly – although the FFT data suggested that she was a middling ability student her CAT quantitative score was very high. If she had been placed in a set on the basis of CATs she would easily have been in the top set.

One day the teacher sat down with Sara and asked about her previous experience of maths and how she felt about the subject. It soon became apparent that she had low self-esteem in the subject (and looking back at her primary school reports it was easy to see why!) and an expectation that she would find things hard to grasp. At this point Sara's teacher shared with her selected high points from the CATs data, including a list of the highest-scoring students on the quantitative test in her year group in order of score with all the names except Sara's blanked out.

He explained that he couldn't just move her into the top set but there was no doubt that she could cope there. All she needed to do was produce the test scores to justify moving her up through the sets.

The seed was sown and by the start of Year 10 Sara was in set 2 of 5. She went on to get a B in maths GCSE. It wasn't the data that made a difference, it was the use of the data by a teacher as a lever to raise her aspirations. The hard work came later but the starting point was the teacher using the data rather than just storing it, and then using it in conjunction with his professional skills and knowledge of his students to make a difference.

Exam analysis

After exam results come in there is always a spell when everyone seems to be analysing and heads of departments will be producing detailed breakdowns of how classes and groups of students performed. This is all well and good but you want to be making formative use of the data for your classes – formative for you as a teacher.

Quantitative data can be used to help you improve your own performance. Be self-critical and don't accept the easy explanations for poor results from students that you have taught – you don't need us to tell you the sorts of excuses that we come up with when a student or class underperform. What could you have done differently that might have had a positive impact? Try to put this into practice the next time you find yourself teaching a similar student or group of students. Analyse your GCSE results rigorously. How did the students do in your subject compared to their performance in other subjects? How does their perform-

analyse your GCSE results rigorously

ance compare to the performance of students in other classes taking the same subject? Which students bucked the trend by performing better than or worse than their peers? How might you account for this? Don't wait for other people to do this kind of analysis for you – learn from your own experience. Perhaps you are doing really well with able girls but able boys are doing less well with you than with one of your colleagues; go and see that colleague at work and talk to him or her about what they think made that difference.

But don't beat yourself up over poor results from your students – learn from those results and try different things next year. Analysing past performance is sterile and pointless if you don't then use that analysis to modify your approach to try to increase student success in the future. The data might say that you have been more or less successful with students or classes than your colleagues – think healthy scepticism and don't feel too proud or too depressed! Why you got those results is the question you want to be considering. Analysis of the data and reflection on the implications can have a really positive effect on the performance of your students in the future.

Some things to ask yourself might include:

- How accurate were my predicted grades? With which groups of students (able boys, less able girls, idle students, Chinese students and so on – be wide-ranging in your definition of a group) was I particularly accurate or inaccurate? How can I adjust my expectations next year and use them to get students to perform better?

- How did students perform from KS2 to KS3 and then on to KS4 or KS5? Which students made particularly good or poor progress at one stage or another? Which students in my current (and future) groups seem likely to repeat this pattern? Use the knowledge to raise aspirations.

- On which questions in the exam did my students do well or badly? (This kind of data is available on some exam board websites.) What does this tell me about what I need to adjust in my teaching of content and exam skills?

Exam analysis for the classroom teacher shouldn't be about competition with colleagues ('My residual was $+2.5$ but hers was only $+2.4$ – what a loser!') but about learning which approaches and strategies worked and which need modification. Formative data analysis is what will make you a more effective teacher in the future.

brilliant recap

- Reflect on the data, don't just file it away or generate it and pass it on. Then use the data to help you see where and how best to apply your professional skills and knowledge.

- Be sceptical about all data, especially quantitative data – use it to generate hypotheses about why things went as they did rather than accepting it at face value. Then test those hypotheses.

- Don't undervalue qualitative data or your own experience.

- Data is neutral, it's how it is used that makes a difference to whether it aids or impedes good teaching and learning.

Summary

General Haig, apparently, could not visit hospitals where he was forced to see the men who had been injured in carrying out his battle plans. It was facing up to the individuals behind the statistics of so many wounded that caused him pain. Data in schools that obscures the stories of the individuals behind it is dangerous because it easily leads us to do things that are good for the data but not necessarily so good for those individuals. Using the data to help improve the aspirations and achievements of individuals should be the aim of the brilliant teacher.

CHAPTER 7

Make it personal: effective methods of differentiation in the classroom

Not another worksheet!

Said by hundreds of children in hundreds of lessons every day

There's a theme running through much of this book – a fairly simple educational philosophy. We want to stress that education is about individuals and that the teacher's job is to help bring the best out of those individuals entrusted to her or his care. And that makes differentiation central because it is about trying to cater for the differences that make individuals unique.

Surprisingly, given the importance of differentiation, there's comparatively little written about it. In fact it is often treated in schools as if it were straightforward and self-evident, but it isn't.

Differentiation is just like assessment for learning – it isn't just a set of procedures, it's about an attitude of mind. It's important that you don't pay lip service to stretching and supporting *the class* but that you are concerned about giving *individuals* what they need to be the best they can. It's about trying to find ways to help individuals to learn, not about thinking that as you've got three different worksheets for a lesson the job has been done. All classes in any subject, whether set, streamed or mixed ability, contain students with differing strengths and weaknesses. The child whose written work is superb but who is almost incapable of speech, the child whose tactical awareness in games is superb but whose hand-eye coordination is poor, the child whose practical abilities are superb but who is unwilling to plan or to evaluate – all of these need a different approach from the teacher to help them achieve their best.

So, at the start, let's be clear: *all* teachers need to differentiate, not just those with mixed ability groups. Sets and streams disguise some of the need for differentiation but they don't do away with it. Many top sets contain students who are working flat out to justify their place in the set whilst others grasp every concept the moment they encounter it. The first group of students need help to reinforce their grasp of the topic, the second need opportunities to deepen their grasp of the topic and to apply their knowledge to new situations. Lower sets will contain students who struggle and others who, through laziness, poor behaviour or whatever, will have sunk through the sets and find the work very straightforward. How the teacher deals with this diversity of need is differentiation.

all teachers need to differentiate

The terms used to designate groups of students are really volatile – what is the modish term one week is, apparently, so-last-year the next. To avoid this we're using the terms *more able* and *less able*. They might be crude and simplistic but at least in a year or so you'll still know roughly what we mean! We're calling a support member of staff working in the classroom with a teacher a teaching assistant (TA).

Ways to differentiate

We've mentioned elsewhere that not being over-reliant on one technique or teaching style is best – flexibility and adaptability are marks of the brilliant teacher – and the same is true of differentiation. You need a wide repertoire of approaches that you can choose from. Always differentiating in the same way will bore the students and make your lessons too predictable.

Here are a few different ways in which you could differentiate work.

Differentiation by support

Some students need a lot of help to accomplish tasks or acquire skills and others need very little. The teacher might provide the support or it might be a teaching assistant or even another student. The support might be as simple as checking that the student has grasped the instructions or periodic checking that everything is going well. The thing that really must be avoided is having the teaching assistant welded to the side of a student with the result that most of the work actually gets done by the TA.

If you've got a task that begins with pair or group discussion and then moves on to individual written work you've already built in a lot of support for the least able and you are requiring the most able to articulate precisely their understanding. All teachers know that it isn't until you start to explain things to others that you discover if you really understood it in the first place!

Differentiation by assessment

You have different expectations of students and you don't react in the same way to different students when they are working on a task or when they complete it. So, you will inject challenge into work at an appropriate level as you move round the class asking questions. When the final product is assessed you respond appropriately to it, not giving a simple mark out of 10 but by praising what has been done well by the student's standards and by offering appropriate criticism. You might be pleased that one student has grasped the basics of the water cycle and might be disappointed that another has let one or two subtleties slip past. Your suggestions of what needs to be done to improve will not be based on an expectation that the next step of learning is the same for all but will be tailored to what the next step is for this particular student.

> inject challenge into work at an appropriate level

Differentiation by task

You assign different tasks to different students, depending on their ability. This often means the following.

Differentiation by worksheet

This is, perhaps, the most common approach to differentiation from diligent teachers. We've seen classes with three or four different worksheets being used to get students working on the same topic. Hours of labour go into this and sometimes this is misplaced because, with targeted support and some thoughtful explanation (deliberately keeping the sentences short and grammatically simple, reading out the sheet to the class, running through key technical terms and getting students to decode the potential difficulties), the teacher could get by with only one or two versions and use the time saved to assess more fully (or even to have a life!). If the needs in your class are so very disparate that four versions of every worksheet are needed then maybe your whole teaching approach needs reconsideration and you should be doing things in such a way that you don't use worksheets with them.

Another danger is that these 'levels' of worksheet (or, in some subjects, of textbook) actually increase the attainment gap by providing challenge, high-level thinking demands and open-ended questions for some but a narrow and more utilitarian focus for others. Less able students need to be developing higher-order thinking skills, too, not just filling in gaps or practising recall.

Differentiation by resource provision

This is a rather more subtle variation on the worksheet approach. The worksheet usually assumes that everyone is learning the same stuff in pretty much the same way at the same time. Resource provision here implies that there are a *range* of resources available and that students may well be working on very different material in very different ways. In the classroom where differentiation by resource is happening, students (or, probably, groups of students) will be doing very different things and the teacher's plans will be less about what happens in a lesson and more about what students will do in three weeks or over half a term. There are likely to be differing levels of minimal expectations for everyone, the teacher will be promoting resources of differing challenge to students and there will be a range of different types of work going on. This approach is relatively costly to set up (in both expense and staff time) but, as something that happens once a year for, say, half a term, it can provide a pleasant contrast to more traditional schemes of work and allows the teacher to spend time having meaningful conversations with individuals rather than dealing with the whole class as if it were one entity.

> this approach is relatively costly to set up

brilliant tip

If you have a particularly enjoyable task, deliberately limit the availability of the resources for it and insist that certain other tasks need to be completed to a satisfactory standard before students' names can be added to the waiting list for the treat. Motivation for completing the more basic work will increase!

Differentiation by outcome

When differentiation gets mentioned this approach usually is denigrated and gets caricatured as simply telling all students what to do and then sitting back until they've done it. Some do it well and some don't. If this were what really happened the critics would be right but, in practice, this rarely happens in school because students will get more or less attention from the teacher, from teaching assistants or from their peers. With a well-designed task, appropriate support while the task is being done and appropriate response afterwards there can be appreciable differentiation going on.

The big danger is that this approach will be adopted for homework tasks where there is no teacher or TA support available. This results in a lot of distress at home for those who experience difficulties and fails to help stretch those who find the task simple. If you find yourself setting the same homework for an entire class then you need to find other ways to make it manageable for all students.

Differentiation by expectation

This is simple but really effective and useful in class, especially if you are setting homework – you set three or four levels of expectation: one for those who find it easy, one for most of the class and one for those who find it tricky. You know which students you need to speak to, reminding them that they *will* find the work easy and will complete it at the highest level.

Your expectations might be as simple as the quantity produced or might be about the ideas you are teaching (the minimum you want everyone to grasp, what you expect most to understand, the extension for the more able and perhaps the super-extension open-ended questions you leave with one or two students).

Differentiation for more able students

Most things that are effective differentiation are really just good practice and will have a positive impact on the learning of all your students and this is never more true than thinking about differentiating work for the most able students in a class. Able students need to be stretched, but isn't that true of all students? Able students need the opportunity to develop higher-order skills (being creative, analysing and synthesising information, being evaluative), but isn't this true of all students? Formative assessment starts with considering what you want students to learn and then thinking about the task and the way students are encouraged to work on it. Differentiation is the same: it's built into what you do from the start and not something that is bolted on at the end as a kind of optional extra. You need to be designing lessons that will allow for students to achieve differently because that will allow all students to achieve highly.

For many teachers differentiation is either giving different work to students, depending on perceived ability, or giving more work to those who finish quickly. It's sad but true that in some classrooms being clever effectively means getting punished – you finish quickly and then just have to do more of the same to reinforce a concept that you grasped first time. Of course, in the classroom where homework is 'to finish off' the bright student gets little or no homework, but that probably is inadequate compensation for being bored and patronised in school.

The most able are not a simply definable group – ability is not like an illness! – and teachers need to be considering the individuals in the class rather than some amorphous

> teachers need to be considering the individuals in the class

bunch. Think, 'What needs to be done to help Isaac or Brier achieve their best?' not 'What task can I tag on to the lesson for those who finish early (or who *should* finish early)?'

⚡ brilliant dos and don'ts

Do

✔ Be widely read in your subject and be willing to recommend books, websites and so on that will challenge students and then discuss the content with them.

▶

✔ Consider constructing the task so that you can point out clearly minimal expectations, expectations for most, extended expectations for a few and optional work for those who like the idea of extending themselves (your job is to motivate more and more students to want to put themselves into this position).

✔ Consider doing fewer short, closed tasks and activities and more open tasks where there are greater possibilities for students to go into greater depth and follow up interests.

✔ Set up activities where a group of students completes a task with each contributing in different ways.

✔ Get an individual or a small group to make themselves expert in something and then teach it to the class.

✔ Make sure that tasks allow for using and developing higher-order skills and then allow for challenging the student to apply or master them.

✔ Tell students how much potential they have as a prelude to a rigorous critique of how they could improve to get closer to reaching that potential.

Don't

✘ Underestimate what *motivated* students can cope with: too often teachers put an artificial ceiling on achievement.

✘ Simply differentiate by task too often – it labels, it demotivates and it often robs those students who are perceived as the least able of the opportunity to try to develop higher-order thinking skills. It also marks out the most able and that is not always something that is welcomed by them.

✘ Be threatened by students who ask questions you can't answer but instead use your greater knowledge to help them discover where to find their own answers.

All teachers know that ability isn't everything and that effort is crucial. We've all seen students with masses of natural talent being over-shadowed by students with greater application. If you neglect your Ferrari, one day the well-maintained and race-tuned Robin Reliant will beat you when you pull away at the lights! One danger of a focus on gifted and talented (G&T) is that there's an arbitrary cut-off and those students who don't quite make it into the G&T group find themselves excluded. This can't be good so don't restrict extension material to just a few – make it available to all who want to try it.

Differentiation for less able students

It's a sad truth that often the most needy students are placed with the least experienced or the least well-qualified staff. Indeed, in some cases they are effectively handed over to the teaching assistant and ignored by the class teacher. Surely, though, one of the greatest challenges in teaching is helping students who find it hard to learn – and isn't this where the best and most experienced teachers should be deployed? It says something about school or departmental ethos when the more you get paid the fewer challenging students you have to encounter.

Another sad truth is that teachers' expectations for less able students tend to be pitched below those students' actual potential, especially in set or streamed classes – what the teacher does is often more concerned with control than with learning. This is understandable but it will result in underachievement.

Liaising with specialist teachers

In most secondary schools these days you will find students with complex needs and it would be foolish to pretend that we can give specialist advice here about dealing with students who are dyspraxic, who have a semantic-pragmatic disorder, who are visually or hearing-impaired and so on. If you find yourself teaching one of these students (and be sure you've checked to find out – schools are not always as good as they might be at disseminating essential information like this), you need to find

find out as much as you can about them and how they learn

out as much as you can about them and how they learn. Liaising with the specialist support staff is essential because they will have expertise or experience that you won't have.

Let's say, for example, that you find you will be teaching a hearing-impaired student – how will this require you to modify your practice? There are complications and subtleties that probably never would occur to you but that a specialist quickly could summarise. There also should be detailed records on file in the school that you will want to read and ask questions about, and you need to get to grips with the practicalities of how, for example, you do class talks with a student who needs to have a clear view of a speaker's lips in order to have a good chance of being able to follow.

Some teachers view the challenge of working with students who find aspects of learning hard as an annoyance or an intrusion into the real job of delivering information – if the kid can't learn like the rest, surely they should be in a special school? We'd encourage you to view the challenge positively and to think about how taking account of all the students' needs is making you a better teacher by widening your repertoire of styles and approaches and how, by considering complex issues about learning difficulties, you will deepen your understanding of the kinds of barriers that teachers need to demolish.

General difficulties

We are concerned here with the broad category of students who find learning in school a challenge. Typically, these students have some or all of these difficulties:

- poor reading and writing skills;
- poor listening skills;

- poor short-term memory;
- short concentration spans;
- difficulty following instructions;
- difficulty grasping abstract concepts;
- a restricted vocabulary.

Like with differentiating for able students, what is good for students with specific difficulties is good for lots of others. So, you might start the lesson by introducing the key vocabulary because otherwise the student will encounter these new words in the lesson and, while they are trying to work out what they mean, the rest of the content will slip by them. How many students simply don't understand what the teacher is saying because so much of the vocabulary is unfamiliar (technical terms, unnecessarily formal language and so on)?

> what is good for students with specific difficulties is good for lots of others

brilliant tip

If you want to introduce vocabulary to a class you could give them a starter where they need to match words and (simple) definitions. Run through this on the board and you've got a basic form of pre-teaching that will reduce confusion when the words occur later.

Accessibility

Simply by making work more accessible to all you can reduce the need for more demanding differentiation strategies. Think about written communication: typeface, use of pictures, readability and presentation through different media.

brilliant dos and don'ts

Do

- ✔ Use lots of pictures and white space. Don't cram stuff in.
- ✔ Check your grammar. Use active sentences rather than passive ('The cat likes tuna' rather than 'Tuna is liked by the cat') and keep the sentences fairly short – try to avoid longer than about 20 words – with no more than one subordinate clause. (Don't restrict yourself to over-short, grammatically simple sentences, though – it looks patronising.)
- ✔ Keep the vocabulary as straightforward as possible (say that cars 'crash' rather than 'collide', for example) and gloss technical terms either in a separate 'word box' or in the text. Science texts seem particularly hard to simplify because the concepts require so much specialist language. If in doubt, introduce fewer new concepts at a time.

Don't

- ✘ Use lots of typefaces in documents – stick to one and don't make it too ornate (Comic Sans is probably the easiest to read).
- ✘ Write in upper case – it's much harder to read a text that is in capitals because all the letters are the same height. The ascenders and descenders of lower case help make it easier to recognise letters.
- ✘ Fully justify the text – keep the right margin ragged so it's easier to keep track of where you are on the page.

Homework

Homework can be a source of real misery for less able students and for their parents. Often the less able can't:

- copy from the board (they can't retain more than a word or two in their memory at a time and then get lost trying to locate where they had got up to);

- write quickly enough from teacher dictation;
- read back their own writing;
- remember what they were told in class;
- remember to take essential resources home;
- do the task without support that isn't available at home.

There are a number of ways round this problem. You could simply not require homework from a student for some or all of the time. The world doesn't end if a student misses out on homework, especially if the difficulties they encounter mean that they spend a disproportionate amount of time on it and that it causes massive ructions at home. A sense of perspective helps here.

Having different homeworks pitched at a lower level for some students can be useful. Yes, they aren't being pushed to the same level as the rest of the class but what's better – doing some work and learning something or being confused and learning nothing?

Other problems are not hard to resolve with some thought and preparation. The teacher can write the homework task down for some students, or a teaching assistant could, or one of the student's friends. To save embarrassment, the student can be issued with a card that asks the teacher to write down the homework task (we've seen this in action very successfully). Actually having the homework instructions duplicated in advance can make a massive difference for students, and it saves time in lessons. Very enterprising

set the homework fairly early in the lesson

teachers or departments have the homework tasks duplicated on sticky labels that can be stuck in planners or in exercise books. Homework tasks can be made available electronically to students and parents. Some of these solutions take a little time but you can look on it as an investment: if the homework task is clearly outlined and saved, you can easily modify it year on year and make it available to colleagues. Whatever you do, set the homework fairly early in the lesson rather than waiting until the last minute as the bell goes and everyone races to pack up!

Using support staff

One of the greatest assets you can have to help you teach effectively is the support of a teaching assistant (TA) and yet all too often the TA is underused or used in an inefficient way.

In some lessons a TA learns a lot but the student they are supporting doesn't. We all know that as teachers we feel threatened by the prospect of our students not performing well and that this leads to us spoon-feeding and neglecting education in favour of training to pass exams. TAs often feel that if a student's work isn't good then this is a reflection on them and, at its worst, this can lead to the TA doing the thinking and the writing for a student; the student becomes totally reliant on the TA and fails to engage with what's going on and doesn't make progress. It's your job as a teacher to ensure that the TA is helping the student learn and this means that you are responsible for managing the way in which the TA works.

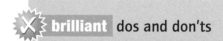 **brilliant** dos and don'ts

Do

✔ Keep the TA informed about what will happen in the lesson as far in advance as you can.

✔ Ask the TA for feedback on your plans and on your lessons.

✔ Actively seek the TA's opinion on what seems to help students – the TA may well have seen them in other classes and with other teachers and will provide useful insights.

✔ Encourage the TA to help all of the students in the room, not just the less able students.

✔ Respect the TA and don't treat them as your dogsbody.

✔ Support the TA so that all students know they must treat them with respect.

Don't

✘ Let the TA do the work for the student.

✘ Expect the TA to make decisions or do jobs that are your responsibility.

One danger of having a TA in the room is that the teacher assumes that it is no longer their job to work with less able students (that's the TA's job!). This is a neglect of duty on the part of the teacher and it needs to be your rule that the less able get a fair share of your attention. Research has suggested that students with support sometimes make less progress than students with similar difficulties and no support and this may well be because when there is no TA the teacher has to spend time with the less able. The TA is there to work with you to help students overcome a barrier to learning, they can't replace you – don't undervalue your own expertise!

brilliant case study

Ms Spenser is the class teacher and Ms Hawk is the teaching assistant. They went through Ms Spenser's plans for the unit of work a few weeks ago and Ms Hawk made some suggestions about things that some students in the class might need to modify and about ways in which those students learned. She also took away a textbook and modified some sections (she didn't come in to support a couple of lessons and did this work then). Ms Spenser has seen those modifications, tweaked them a little and they have both agreed on them.

In the lesson Ms Spenser explains the work to the class while Ms Hawk moves around the room helping students to stay focused on the instructions. Once the task begins both adults check that students know what they are to do and then move away. One table of students is rather ▶

unsettled and Ms Hawk moves over to them to make sure that they stay on task while Ms Spenser asks one of the less able students some questions to check that he has grasped the implications of the work. He hasn't and she redefines in simpler terms what they are doing, drawing other students from the table into the discussion. While this is going on several students have put up their hands for help and Ms Hawk goes to them. Most of the questions are simple process questions, two content questions she can help with because she knew what was coming up this lesson and has read the chapter on it already (one of the questions she had raised herself before the lesson and Ms Spenser was able to explain things to her so she can now pass on the explanation). There is one question that is beyond her but a quick glance shows that Ms Spenser is still helping the student with conceptual difficulties so Ms Hawk gets the table involved in a discussion, admitting she isn't too sure of the answer.

The class are used to working this way. They know that either adult will work with any student or group of students and have no objection to it. They know that Ms Hawk has the same disciplinary power as Ms Spenser and that, if she doesn't always have the same subject knowledge, she knows how to help them find the answers for themselves, just like Ms Spenser does. Both adults work as a team.

At the end of the lesson the adults briefly reflect on what happened. Ms Spenser isn't certain that all of the students grasped the central point of what she was trying to do and wonders how to reinforce it; Ms Hawk suggests she has a word with Mr Silverman – he used an effective technique in a lesson a week or two back that she thinks might be adaptable to the concept and the class.

The adults have worked together to help all students learn and to assess that learning.

Personalisation – knowing individuals

By necessity we've had to talk about methods and about techniques as if these were things that existed in a vacuum but, of course, we're talking about classes made up of individuals and it's worth taking time to think about what is the best way you should intervene with those individuals to get the most out of them. Challenge some too much and they will give up; build in competition for some and they will respond positively. Keep reminding yourself that your key skill as a teacher is managing the individuals in your classes, not simply applying a range of teaching techniques with greater or lesser efficiency. Knowing your students well and reflecting on your experiences will mean that your responses will grow more subtle over time and more learning will happen in your lessons. It may start with crude terms like 'more able' or 'less able' but, in the end, good differentiation *personalises* learning and that recognition of the individual is what will produce the longest lasting effect.

 brilliant recap

- Plan for differentiation – it's at the heart of your work as a teacher.

- Consciously widen your repertoire of approaches to differentiation – keep trying to think of new ways to do it in order to keep it fresh for you and the students.

- Make the most of support from specialist teachers and teaching assistants – their insights are informed by knowledge that you almost certainly don't have.

- Keep thinking about accessibility of work – often simple things can make a big difference to a student's ability to cope.

Summary

This isn't the last word on differentiation – how could it be? Every year will bring new students with new challenges and at times having to make special provision can seem like a chore, but remember that differentiation is about recognising the unique qualities that every student brings with them. As you become more skilled at planning for all students to learn you become a better teacher.

CHAPTER 8

On top of the form: the role of the form tutor

Great teachers empathise with kids, respect them, and believe that each one has something special that can be built upon.

Ann Lieberman

n many ways the relationship that a student has with their form tutor is the most important of all. As a form tutor you will meet with your tutees daily and be in a stronger position than others to influence them. Being a form tutor is one of the most rewarding and interesting aspects of any teacher's job and we would strongly recommend that you embrace this position wholeheartedly as, in many ways, this is what you will have come into education for. You will be the person who has first contact every morning with the individuals in your form and will be able to determine what mood they are in, whether they are experiencing relationship problems and how they are coping in various subjects. More importantly, however, you will be the one who can shape their day. A good form tutor can make a massive difference to the life chances of an individual and is often the person people look back on when they leave school as being the one who helped them most.

you will be the one who can shape their day

The aim of this chapter is to consider the various roles carried out by form tutors and to suggest ways to make your life as a tutor both manageable and enjoyable. Finally, be prepared. This is a very practical chapter and will require your active involvement. Many of the tasks ask you to examine various scenarios and consider your actions. The intention is to make it stimulating as well as informative.

Duties of the tutor

Study the list below and ask yourself how many of these are *legal* requirements and how many are expectations of a good tutor.

Assemblies	Collecting reply slips
Recording rewards	Completing reports
Registration	Holding detentions
Recording set changes	One-to-one reviewing
Checking homework diaries	Contacting parents
Arranging visits	Collecting money
Organising fundraising	Checking uniform
Electing form officials	Checking unauthorised absences
Counselling	Form meetings
Monitoring progress	Clarifying school rules

In fact, the only legal requirement you have is to take a register. However, if this was all tutors did schools would be very poor places indeed! The reality is significantly different. As a form tutor you are expected to carry out many of the functions above and therefore have to work out strategies to ensure that you not only cope, but also become a brilliant form tutor.

brilliant timesaver

We want to start by giving you an excellent way to save time. Just remember three letters: *SEP* – somebody else's problem. Whenever you come across issues to be dealt with, ask yourself, who should be dealing with them – you or someone else? If it is you then that's fine, but if it is the job of somebody else, give it to them and remember *SEP*.

Take another look at the list above and perhaps even add other duties you might care to think of. Next to each one place a tick if you feel it is the duty of the form tutor to do this. If you think it is the duty of someone else put the letters *SEP* next to it. For example, if one of your tutees is given a detention in history you might want to be informed about it, but you would certainly not be expected to administer it, unless, of course, you are their history teacher as well as their form tutor! When one of your tutees is moved up or down a set in maths (or any other subject for that matter), should you be the person who records this? As a caring tutor you might want to know about it, but it is not your responsibility to actually change the school records. Also, you would not be expected to arrange a trip for your form if it was to do with a subject you did not teach. Being aware of the duties you can pass on straight away is an essential feature for anyone who aspires to be a brilliant form tutor. You will not have the time to do all of these things even if you wanted to. One of the first things that we would advocate, therefore, is the use of *SEP*. This is something we will return to later in the chapter.

Meeting the parents

One of the most successful ways a form tutor can operate is by getting to know the parents or guardians of their tutees. We strongly recommend that, as a tutor, you make this a priority, if at all possible. The chances are, apart from parents' evening, that you will not need to meet many of the parents of your charges. However, if you do have to contact a parent or guardian for any reason, a relationship that has already been established makes things all the easier. It is also important that parents feel they are involved in the school life of their son or daughter. Remember that for some parents or guardians school was a nightmare and is not necessarily a place they feel comfortable in. With this is mind it is important that every effort is made to put them at their ease. Due to the fact that we have greater access to technology than ever before, you can make contact through emails and text messages as well as by phone. The following case study illustrates just this point and demonstrates the effect that a positive relationship between the tutor and the parent can have on the student.

⤢ brilliant case study

Mr Woodard was an experienced form tutor in a mixed 11–18 comprehensive and had just been given responsibility for a new Year 7 class. Understandably, some of the parents were anxious about their children settling in and wanted reassurance from Mr Woodard that all was fine. One of the parents in particular said her son, Dean, who was somewhat boisterous, was being called names by some children in Year 9 and was reluctant to come to school. Dean's descriptions of the boys were very vague and changed three times.

Mr Woodard talked to Dean about the incident and showed him photographs of the Year 9 group. Dean, for one reason or another, could not or would not identify the students concerned. After spending some time on the case, Mr Woodard phoned Dean's mum to inform her that the situation was being dealt with, but that Dean had not identified any boys. Dean's mum was very grateful for the time Mr Woodard had spent and was much more reassured about Dean's welfare at school, particularly the way in which her concerns were addressed.

Later on in the year Dean was involved in a number of incidents which led to him being given one day's internal exclusion. Because Mr Woodard had made initial contact with Dean's mum it made it easier for him to liaise with her and convince her this was the right thing for the school to do. Dean's mum was not best pleased about her son's fate, but trusted the decision of the school because of the time invested by the form tutor.

Clearly, it would be naïve to believe that every parent would react in the same way that Dean's mum did. However, the point being made is that the relationship between the form tutor and the parents or guardians of the students is an essential one and, if nurtured properly, could prove to be very fruitful indeed.

Being a form tutor is unique and very different from the other demands that may be placed on you as a classroom teacher. Many of your duties will be administrative tasks, such as signing diaries or ensuring letters are given out and actually get home. Effective use of form time will allow the tutor to get through many of these tasks efficiently, leaving time to be far more creative, focusing on getting to know your form as individuals, target setting, organising assemblies or celebrating achievement. Using the brilliant tip below will allow you to carry out many of the administrative duties without fuss whilst also giving you time to catch up with students in your form.

brilliant tip

The time you spend with your form will vary according to the school you are in. Typically form tutors will see their forms about three times a week in the classroom and perhaps twice a week in assembly. At some point they may have a form period in which the tutor delivers the PSHE period or has time with their form to use how they see fit. Most schools have organised programmes. What we have found to be particularly useful is if, during the shorter 10- or 15-minute meetings, students are required either to read or to complete homework in silence. The form tutor can then get on with the job of checking diaries, or calling individuals to the front and having short meetings with them regarding incidents that may have happened in school or discussing their progress in various subjects – mentoring, in effect. They may simply want to see how the student's weekend went!

It is also your responsibility to set the tone for the day. This includes encouraging a positive attitude, correcting or positively commenting on

▶

uniform and preparing your students for the challenges of the day. A positive form tutor can often change the way a student sees the day. The aim is to get your form into the habit of coming in and getting out their homework or reading. You yourself can get together a collection of books or magazines that you can give to those who turn up without a book. The secret is to be well organised and establish routines.

Using form time effectively

As well as delivering the PSHE programme you may be in a fortunate position where you get to spend regular time with your form. Often tutors are not sure what to do and find that the time goes by without any significant development of the form in terms of issues or relationships. Below is a variety of suggestions that you can put into place immediately that will enable you to make the most of your form time.

- *Show and tell.* This is geared mainly towards Years 7–9 but can, on occasions, work with older students. This is an opportunity for any of your tutees to bring in items they are interested in or talk about personal achievements. Schools are busy places in which students will not always have the opportunity to discuss what motivates them or what their interests are, so it is a great way of allowing them to do this. Also it is a fantastic way for you as a tutor to get to know your students in a much deeper way.

- *Hidden talents.* This is very much like show and tell but students are encouraged to write things down rather than speak to the class. This activity gives you an insight into students' lives outside of the classroom, what they would like to do if given the opportunity and if there is something they are really good at that the school doesn't know about. The tutor gives the students a sheet of paper with the following three questions on:

(a) Out of school, what are you interested in?

(b) Is there something you'd like to do at school that you've never had the opportunity to do? If so, what?

(c) Is there something you know you're really good at that we don't know about? If so, what is it?

It is surprising what the students come up with and it allows you to tune into them to a greater degree. It may also provide you and other colleagues with ideas on how to motivate particular students during lessons.

- *Top of the form.* As mentioned earlier, being a form tutor is unique and provides you with an opportunity to really get to know your form. Over time they will also get to know you and see you as *theirs.* One way of raising self-esteem is to keep a book of positive comments about every member of your form. Give each form member a piece of paper with the names of every other student on. Beside each name they need to write one positive comment. It might be as simple as, 'She is kind to everyone in the class.' At the end of the exercise collect in all the pieces of paper. You then can do a number of things with them. You could type up the comments for each student and give them to him or her. Or, if this seems too onerous, you could read out regularly the comments to the form. Whatever you decide to do this is a fantastic way of making your students feel good and an excellent way of bonding.

- *Target setting.* This is particularly useful for GCSE/A-level students, but should be used for those lower down the school as well. Whilst the rest of the form is completing homework, reading or engaged in other activities, you can talk to one student at a time. These meetings do not necessarily have to be that long (a quick check might take only five minutes). This is an opportunity for you to discuss with the student aspects of a subject they think they are good at and to offer them strategies for perceived weaknesses. It is particularly useful when, as a form tutor, you write tutor reports. You can use these conversations as a basis for how the student feels they are progressing. Again, they are opportunities for you to catch up with things the student is interested in and to strengthen relationships.

- *Assemblies.* In many schools, form groups are required to devise and to carry out assemblies. Use of the form time is a good way to make this happen. Some tutors may feel brave and allow their form to organise it without their input, but it is often the case that you will have to coordinate it. Again, this is a superb way for students to display the talents they have beyond the classroom. Additionally, you will, at times, be surprised to see the quieter members of your form revealing their hidden talents!

- *Form reps reporting back.* Today almost every school will have an active school council and it is likely that students from your form will attend the year council meetings. Form time can be a useful way of encouraging your form to discuss the issues they want the reps to take forward and for the reps to feed back progress. Try to organise it so that this does not become a moaning session, but is a practical way for your form to take part in whole-school decision making.

- *Hear my voice.* Introduce students to the dying art of public speaking. Show them film clips of great public speakers and encourage them to hold debates. Spend time analysing and discussing the techniques needed for effective speaking and give students the opportunities to put these into practice.

- *Coaching.* Students of all ages are under intense pressure to perform. The demands of everyday life are greater than ever and we live in an ever changing world where some of the jobs your students will do have not even been invented yet! What many students need is someone to be on their side and to be there for them. The form tutor as a coach is a really powerful way of developing the interpersonal skills of your students as well as getting them to consider how they perform best both inside and outside of the classroom. Again, this depends on time but, if possible, speak to members of your form individually. Occasionally you might even need to explain to some students what good listening is (e.g. model sitting up straight and being attentive alongside positive use of eye contact).

None of the above suggestions is compulsory in any way. However, the role of the form tutor is extremely rewarding if carried out with care and conviction. Students will know if you genuinely care about them or are just going through the motions. The ability to communicate effectively and create an environment of mutual trust will go a long way in making you a brilliant form tutor, as will showing unconditional love and a sense of fairness.

Problem solving 1

As a form tutor you will be asked to solve a number of problems regarding your tutees. Some of these complaints might come from parents or colleagues who feel you need to get a grip on your form. In this part of the chapter we will present you with a variety of situations. The first ones involve parents and we would like you to consider what your responses might be to the following situations. Underneath each scenario briefly jot down your reaction. Remember to ask yourself if 'somebody else's problem' (SEP) applies.

1   A parent of one of your form writes a note to you in the homework diary to complain that history homework has not been set for six weeks.

2   It is period 1. You have a full teaching day. You have just started to teach when a note from the school office arrives to tell you that a parent of one of your tutor group is in reception and wants to speak to you urgently.

3 A parent writes to you to say that their daughter's mobile phone was stolen at school the day before.

4 A parent emails you complaining that their son's maths teacher had given him a lunchtime detention yesterday and their son had been deprived of lunch as a result.

Possible solutions

1

- Initially check the homework diary of another student in your class to see whether it simply has not been written down.

- If the homework has indeed not been set, this is a SEP issue. Either have a quiet word with the member of staff concerned or pass it on to their head of department.

- Contact the parent to inform them that it is being dealt with.

2

- Remember, you cannot leave the class unattended.

- Send a message back via a student (or you may have a phone in your classroom or, indeed, your pocket!) asking the parent either to make an appointment or to wait until break when you can see them.

- If it is that urgent, try to get a message to the head of year/house or another member of senior staff explaining to them the situation and asking whether they could meet the parent or cover for you whilst you do so. They could then feed back to you the situation. It may be that it has to be referred to the head of year or child protection officer anyway and then it becomes a SEP issue.

- If you are unable to meet the parent, contact them anyway to reassure them that you are aware of the situation.

3

- With this one it could become a SEP issue almost immediately. Many schools have a policy of no mobile phones or require that they be switched off during lessons. Schools repeatedly are requesting that parents do not allow their children to take electronic equipment into school and, if they do, it is at their own risk.

- You may decide to spend some time investigating it or at least pass it on to the head of year/house but, sadly, this type of incident is increasing in schools and there simply is not the time for the form tutor to deal with them. It might be just as profitable to ask the parent to refer the matter to the police, depending on your school policy.

- Again, take the matter seriously whatever you decide to do. It is a very real and worrying incident for parents to deal with.

4

- Remember, all students need to be given time for lunch, even if it is only 15 minutes. Look into the situation by talking to the member of staff concerned or their head of department. It has become a SEP issue.

- Contact the parent to inform them the matter is being dealt with.

Note – with all of the above we would advise you to contact the parent/guardian as a matter of courtesy. As we pointed out earlier, the quality of the relationship between form tutor and parent/guardian is extremely important and sends a strong message to the student about the notion of partnership. There are more complaints from parents about lack of communication than there are criticising staff.

Problem solving 2

Read through the following list of incidents.

- *Incident 1.* A member of your form is being threatened by a group of older students in the school.

- *Incident 2.* You have received repeated complaints about both work and behaviour, from a number of subject teachers, about a member of your form.

- *Incident 3.* A member of your form has been caught smoking in the playground.

- *Incident 4.* A member of your form has started wearing an extremely short skirt and has been using explicitly sexual language, particularly in front of male teachers.

- *Incident 5.* A parent arrives, without an appointment, catches you outside your classroom and tells you that another member of the form is trying to sell illegal substances to their son/daughter.

- *Incident 6.* The parent of a member of your form has complained to you about another member of staff's attitude towards their son/daughter and they are also questioning his/her ability to teach the subject and manage the class.

Now decide for each incident if your action will be one of the following.

A – Record the incident for information, but take no immediate action.

B – Deal with the incident yourself.

C – Consult with your head of year/house and then deal with the incident yourself.

D – Consult with your head of year/house and then jointly deal with the incident.

E – Pass the incident straight away to your head of year/ house or another member of staff for action.

With the exception of incident 4 we have deliberately not provided solutions as we would like you to think them through. (With incident 4 you would want to notify the child protection officer in your school.) It is probably a good idea to discuss your decisions with a colleague and consider the pros and cons of each action you might take. Whatever you decide, remember that you are not alone. The structures in the school are designed to allow you to call upon support when you see fit.

> remember that you are not alone

Problem solving 3

Now look at the type of complaints you may receive from colleagues and, once again, decide what your course of action may be.

- 'I have received no German homework from Callum and he has not been to apologise.'

- 'Please remind Gemma that her geography coursework deadline is Tuesday. She constantly forgets.'

- 'Tazeem has brought no ingredients for food technology. This is the third week in a row. The faculty cannot afford to keep subsidising him.'

- 'Jordan said that he handed his textiles file in with the other students, but I have not received it. This is the second time this year.'

- 'Tayla poured water over Victoria's work and they started fighting. I will not have Tayla in my lesson again unless she can behave.'

- 'Torin arrived at PE without a kit or a note. He says you have the note.'

- 'During art Remy was flicking some paint around and has damaged some of the coursework.'

- 'Mary was late for drama again. This is now causing problems for the others in her group.'

Once again, consider your actions carefully. It is not your responsibility to deal with incidents that occur within the classroom. That is the job of the teacher responsible for that subject. In most schools now subject incidents are referred to the subject leader, though, again, you might want to know for information. If a student is continually coming to your attention then you might want to put them on some kind of monitoring report. If they have got to a stage whereby your influence is no longer sufficient then the monitoring needs to be conducted by the head of year/house.

Celebrating achievement

As a form tutor you are dealing with a mixture of individuals who will have a host of differing interests and backgrounds. That is the beauty of being a form tutor: no two individuals are the same and each person needs to be handled in a different way. We are very quick at labelling students in today's society, but in some ways many of our youngsters conform very well to certain labels and we have to treat them accordingly (see Figure 8.1). This idea of labelling comes from Professor Mick Waters who is President of the Curriculum Foundation (a not-for-profit organisation run by volunteers with the conviction that there is a universal core at the heart of every successful curriculum), and it serves as a useful way of reminding us of the rich tapestry of those whom we serve. The one thing they will share in common, however, will be that they will be members of your form. This final section is intended to provide you with strategies to recognise the strengths of your form, both as a whole and as individuals.

Figure 8.1 The mixed bag

Source: © Mick Waters

Ways of celebrating achievement

- *Displays.* How much of your wall space is dedicated to your form? Not just rotas, reminders of clubs, but actual achievements? Make your form room a home from home where your students feel welcome. Allow them to bring in certificates to show achievements outside of school (e.g. martial arts successes or piano exams). It is not necessarily a good idea to bring in the real certificates, but good-quality photocopies will be just as effective. You can also use wall space to display such things as poetry or artwork. Indeed, if you have someone in the form who is good at art, why not get them to design a form badge or coat of arms?

- *Rewards.* A great way of bonding with your form is to reward them. This can be as ambitious as arranging a trip at the end of term or laying on a Christmas party in the form room. For either of these activities you will, almost certainly, need permission from a senior member of staff, but why not invite them along as well? Other rewards, such as best attendance, highest amount of merits or credits are also ways of recognising achievement or effort. You could even introduce student of the week, whereby someone in your form is recognised for a good deed of some kind. Skilfully done, this will provide you with a way of making sure every member of the form gets recognised in some way or another.

- *Guest speakers.* Why not try to arrange for guest speakers to come and speak to your form? The issues can be wide ranging from the importance of the environment to religious beliefs. As a form you can draw up a list of things you might find interesting and then make an effort to make it happen.

Things we need to remember

The purpose of education is to change lives and, if this is to be done successfully, we must recognise our role in educating the whole child. This is the opportunity we are provided with as a form tutor. Being able to help the students in your care will give you a great feeling and, for some of them, you will be a godsend as they know you will be a regular feature in their life. The

> the purpose of education is to change lives

following statements were 10 key messages that students wanted to get across to teachers at the Youth Parliament Conference in 2009. We would do well to take them seriously.

- Teach us how to talk in a variety of situations.
- Don't spoon-feed us.
- Nobody asks us difficult enough questions.
- Teach us how to transfer skills.
- We do not need to be tested to find out how well we are doing.
- We need to learn life skills, but please don't test us on them.
- Stop teaching to exams – we think the world is bigger than this.
- Get rid of the hierarchy of subjects where some subjects have more status than others.
- Give us teachers with a passion for their subject.
- Stop thinking that everything can be taught ... some things we just have to learn for ourselves.

Becoming a brilliant form tutor will require effort and perseverance. Whilst to some the skills required may come naturally, others may have to work that bit harder. Try to act on the advice given in the brilliant recap overleaf. You are well on the way to becoming a brilliant form tutor!

 **brilliant** recap

- Show your students that you care about them. Often you will be the one they remember when they leave school.

- Make the effort to get to know what they are interested in. One great example is of a form tutor who knew one of his students was in the cast of the West End production *Joseph*; not only did he go to see the production, but he arranged for the form to see it as well.

- Build relationships with parents and guardians. On many occasions these will prove invaluable and enable you to resolve situations in everyone's interests.

- Don't attempt to solve the discipline problems of all members of staff that teach your form. Being aware and having the odd quiet word is sufficient.

- Don't allow the more confident members of the form to dominate – the quiet ones need your attention just as much and your belief in them can do wonders to build their self-esteem.

- Don't underestimate the impact of celebrating achievement. Most members of your form will want to be identified as being in a successful team and this is an excellent reason for arranging activities that allow your form to bond.

Summary

Finally, people who:

- push back the boundaries
- go beyond limits
- live on the edge
- achieve perfection
- are brilliant but unpredictable
- appeal to some but upset others
- have big ideas

are students in your form!

CHAPTER 9

Talk to the heart: managing yourself and others

Any person capable of angering you becomes your master, he can anger you only when you permit yourself to be disturbed by him.

Epictetus

Over the last eight chapters we have explored many of the qualities that will be essential for you to become a highly competent teacher, but your ability to control yourself and effectively deal with others will determine the extent to which you are truly effective. Whilst Chapters 2 and 4 concentrated very much on managing students' behaviour, this chapter is different in the sense that it is about how *you* manage your own emotions alongside those of others, including other adults in the workplace, and will discuss strategies that may enable you to get the best out of everyone you come into contact with. The need for a teacher to be emotionally intelligent is perhaps greater now than at any time previously and there are demands not just in the classroom, but also in the staffroom. As we work our way through the chapter there will be many opportunities for you to consider how you react to differing situations. What is most important, however, is that you keep in mind the importance of developing your awareness of how our emotions can affect us for good or ill.

What is emotional intelligence?

Over the past three decades or so it has become widely recognised that the success of an individual is determined not just by their levels of traditional intelligence, such as memory skills and problem solving, but also by their ability to assess, manage and control their own emotions as well as those of others and groups. Perhaps the most recent popular proponent of emotional intelligence (EI) has been Daniel Goleman, and whilst there are those who criticise his work, he remains one of the most outstanding and widely respected names in the field of EI. Two of his key works are *Emotional Intelligence* (1996) and *The New Leaders* (2002) which he co-authored with Richard Boyatzis and Annie McKee. Goleman's theories relating to EI are targeted primarily at leadership and emphasise four main strands.

1 *Self-awareness.* The ability to understand your own emotions and recognise their impact while using gut feelings to guide decisions.

2 *Self-management.* Involves controlling one's emotions and impulses and adapting to changing circumstances.

3 *Social awareness.* The ability to sense, understand and react to others' emotions while comprehending social networks.

4 *Relationship management.* The ability to inspire, influence and develop others while managing conflict.

Whether you are in your first or thirtieth year in teaching, much of what goes on in the classroom is indeed about leadership, and the ability to lead oneself is arguably the most significant attribute you can develop. It takes only a glance at effective historical and

> the ability to lead oneself is arguably the most significant attribute you can develop

contemporary leaders to see how they have used their emotions to full advantage. Names like Martin Luther King, Winston Churchill, JFK, Tony Blair and Barack Obama are all associated with charisma and the ability to win people over. All of them understood the importance of appealing to the emotions as an integral aspect of their leadership skills and this is what effective teachers do on a daily basis.

In a similar way, but even more recently, schools have been developing programmes that specifically look at the social and emotional aspects of learning in order to manage student behaviour more effectively, whilst enabling youngsters to understand the ways in which their differing emotional states can impact upon them. The key difference here is that we are focusing primarily on how you as the teacher can understand and act upon the differing emotions you may experience and how this impacts upon your classroom practice.

 **activity**

Welcome to your world!

This activity is designed for you to think carefully about what makes you you. We are all affected by our natural temperament as well as external influences, and the greater our awareness of our own character traits the higher the chances we will have of managing them appropriately. For this exercise mark yourself from 1–5 in relation to how you regard yourself (1 and 5 being high indicators of the various traits).

Your natural temperament – mark yourself

Optimistic	1	2	3	4	5	Pessimistic
Risk taker	1	2	3	4	5	Cautious
Unrushed	1	2	3	4	5	Short fuse
Impulsive	1	2	3	4	5	Over-calculating

Once you have done this yourself it is worthwhile asking someone who knows you well to rate you on the same traits and to compare results. Being aware of how you are perceived by others is a vital ingredient of any influential individual.

Now look at the list overleaf and think about how each factor may affect your emotions. Again, these are things we do not often consider, but they can have a positive or negative impact.

▶

- Sunny day/cloudy or rainy day.
- New class group.
- Ofsted in.
- Feeling unwell.
- Good sleep/broken sleep.

These may appear trivial, but it is surprising how often you might hear someone comment on good weather and how it makes them feel better. Knowing what factors contribute to your own moods can have a significant bearing on how your day goes – or doesn't!

Taming your emotions

In Chapter 4 we told you about Eddie and the advice he gave for never getting wound up. In many ways this is much easier said than done, especially if you are a new teacher and are considered 'fresh meat' by some of your new charges. Having an awareness of the science behind the emotions, even on a basic level, whilst not guaranteeing that you will never get agitated again, can be beneficial in that at least you are beginning to understand why you and others around you may react in a certain way. There are times when your emotions can take control over your actions to the extent that you may find it difficult to react in a rational way. For example, a conversation between two or more people who are decidedly passionate about what they are discussing may get heated and, in some cases, may lead to one person saying something they later regret. At this stage their emotions are in control and possibly they have undergone what is known as an 'amygdala hijack', a term coined by Daniel Goleman in his book *Emotional Intelligence* (1996).

The diagram of the human brain, shown in Figure 9.1, shows the journey from sensation to action. Whatever the sensation is, be it vision or sound, it is directed to the thalamus, which

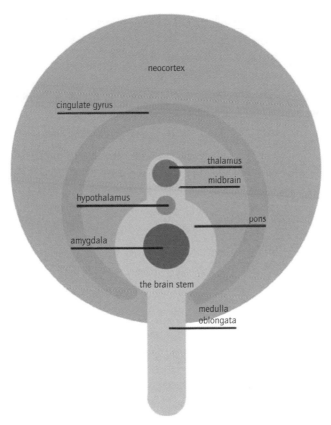

Figure 9.1 The limbic system
Source: © Burkey Belser, Greenfield/Belser, Ltd

is similar to an air traffic controller in that it keeps the signals moving. In most cases the thalamus sends the sensation to the neocortex for processing. The cortex 'assesses' the sensation and makes sense of it. Anything it feels it should get excited by is sent to the amygdala, which releases chemicals known as peptides and hormones to create emotion and consequent action. However, when, to use Goleman's term, 'The hijacking of the amygdala' occurs, the thalamus reacts in a different way. In what it sees as emergencies, the thalamus bypasses the thinking brain, the cortex, and the sensation is sent straight to the amygdala. In times of stress or anger this protects the body but can force an inappropriate response and one that might later be regretted. The 'hijack' process itself essentially shuts down the neocortex one process at a time and prevents logical thinking. In doing so it also prepares the individual for what is known as 'fight or flight'. It releases muscle stimulants, such as adrenaline and caffeine, and the muscles begin to tense in response. At the same time the heart rate increases, as does body temperature, which leads to sweating. The varying solutions a person usually can think of diminish and make it difficult to get through the situation.

The consequences of a hijack

● Once hijacked, chemicals meant for fighting/fleeing are released into the bloodstream and can take between 20 and 40 minutes to dissipate. During this time the thought processes remain shut down and therefore *no effective learning can take place.*

● Usually, the individual cannot fight or flee, so frustration increases, leading to insecurity. Some individuals enjoy this rollercoaster 'buzz', but they are out of control and certainly not able to think straight.

● Two people hijacked can result in a head-to-head argument, perhaps in a fight, which could lead to both personal injury and emotional exclusion. It may be that neither person understands their feelings or remembers their actions. It is easy not to face what you may not understand.

● The effects of the 'hijack' vary in terms of length from one person to another. However, we know it can take between half an hour and three or four hours for the 'fight or flight' emotions to dissipate.

💡 brilliant example

You will be familiar with phrases such as, 'He just snapped...' or 'I can't remember much ... I just lost it.' This often will be a result of a person suffering from an amygdala hijack. One very famous example of this was the tennis player, John McEnroe, in the 1980s. The phrase 'You cannot be serious' became synonymous with him, as he argued continually with umpires if he disagreed with their decisions. So much so that he became a caricature of himself and provided comedians with unlimited material.

Another example can be seen in one of our own experiences at secondary school. Mr X was a cover teacher that appeared to dread coming to school. The fact was that every time he came into the classroom the more boisterous individuals would go out of their way to goad him and, on one occasion, he finally snapped. After putting up with what seemed like months of provocation, one boy flicked a plastic cube at the back of his neck. In an instant he seized the boy by the neck and began to strangle him. The teacher next door was summoned quickly and had to act fast in order to calm the situation. Though this is an extreme example and would, more than likely, result in some form of suspension, if not dismissal, today, it does reveal the effect that an amygdala hijack can have. Once again, after the event, the teacher recognised that he had lost control and was full of remorse.

Understanding that amygdala hijacks can happen goes some way to explaining why some people do indeed 'lose it' and will also help when it comes to managing student anger. There is some evidence to suggest that students with emotional and behavioural difficulties are often victims of a hijack. It must be a welcoming thought for any teacher that this process can be understood and the behaviour can be managed.

Preventing a hijack

To minimise the chances of a hijack it is important to be aware of the emotional factors that can trigger such an event. For example, individuals will be more at risk when they are involved in something they are highly motivated about, if they are overtired or have recently been under stress. The first step in slowing down an attack is to stop and consider the stimulus that may cause the hijack so that the neo-cortex remains involved; the ability to acknowledge the source of the problem can ensure that the neo-cortex continues to play a central part in retaining rational thoughts. It is beneficial if long and deep breaths are taken as they can focus the person. Finally, taking time to reflect afterwards on the factors that triggered the emotions, and learning from this, is essential to prevent a future amygdala hijack from happening.

> it is important to be aware of the emotional factors

 activity

Know your stimulants

1 Take a minute to think about the stimulants that affect your own mood. For each of the senses try to think of examples that have an adverse reaction on you and those that have a calming effect. Having greater self-awareness regarding your emotions will enable you to remain in control, as well as making you more acutely aware when you are beginning to become agitated.

	Sound	Sight	Touch	Taste	Smell
Raises tension					
Induces calm					

2 Try to think of one specific time (the more recent the better) when you might have experienced an amygdala hijack and one when you managed to contain it.

- What were the factors that made you more susceptible to attacks?
- Are there any patterns or triggers you can identify? (For example, a class being exceptionally noisy.)
- What maintained it?
- What did you do to avoid it?

Some people enjoy the aroma of coffee filling a room; others deplore the sound of loud music. As individuals we have different triggers for our emotions. Engaging in positive thoughts or recalling fond memories are also regarded as ways in which the amygdala can be soothed. The secret is knowing yourself and being able to read others, most usefully being the students you teach.

the secret is knowing yourself and being able to read others

brilliant tip

Try to select a positive emotional memory that you can use in the event of calming yourself down. It may be a family picture on an extremely enjoyable holiday or an image of your partner or children. Whatever you choose, make sure there are positive thoughts associated with it. Having a positive attitude and focusing on the good things in your life are known methods a person can use to avoid becoming too agitated. Exercise also helps in ridding the body of any excess adrenaline and can stop the amygdala from taking control. In fact, exercise can assist in thinking becoming more rational.

In many cases throughout your career, some of the students you teach will be subjected to an amygdala hijack and will be even more vulnerable than you. They may not understand the effect of their emotions on their behaviour and will not necessarily have the skills to prevent it from happening. The social and emotional aspects of learning, which might be delivered through the form tutor sessions or separate PSHE periods, if done seriously, can go a long way in enabling youngsters not just to understand the emotions they are experiencing, but also to manage them appropriately.

 **brilliant** activity

One day at school

The purpose of this activity is to reflect upon what you have read so far and how the following two scenarios may affect your day. If possible, complete the exercise with a partner and discuss the possible impact of both.

Scenario one

- You slept poorly, ate too late and are feeling under the weather.
- You get up late and are unable to shower.
- You snap at your partner about something trivial.
- The weather is cold and wet outside.
- You drive to school – the traffic is bad.
- You encounter a motorcyclist and engage in 'road rage'.
- You arrive late and take over your form from the Deputy Head who has stepped in.
- The form is lively. You shout to get their attention. Some have already left for first lesson.
- You put a starter on the board for the first lesson.
- As the class is about to settle you notice their poor attire and it's annoying.
- And you notice a fight starting just outside your room.

How are you likely to deal with the fight, considering the context?

Scenario two

- You exercised last night and enjoyed a good sleep.
- You wake shortly before the alarm.
- You exchange a pleasant word with your partner before you get in the shower.
- You relax over coffee and a croissant – the smell – ahh!
- It is a warm spring day outside and you feel the freshness.
- You drive to school – the traffic is clear.
- On arrival at school you are greeted warmly by the Deputy Head, who smiles at you and says, 'Great lesson yesterday'.
- Though your form activity is challenging, you are encouraged to see your students interacting really well.
- You dismiss them after completing the register and begin to welcome your first class.
- You smile as you see your students straighten their uniforms as they approach your classroom.
- They settle down into the starter.
- And you notice a fight starting just outside your room.

How are you likely to deal with the fight, considering the context?

Dealing with 'challenging adults'

For some of us it is not just the students we may find challenging but other adults as well. Feeling secure in our working relationships is a vital part of success and allows us to carry out our roles effectively. Alternatively, coming up against colleagues or parents who make our lives difficult can lead to misery and underperformance. Whether you are a newly qualified teacher or the subject leader, dealing with people you perceive as 'difficult' will be a reality at some time or another in your career, and the more senior you become the more frequent this seems to be. This section focuses on what we understand by the term 'challenging adults' and considers ways in which we can develop strategies to enhance relationships.

How should we define 'challenging adults'?

In practical terms a 'challenging adult' can be seen as anyone you are in contact with at work that you believe is preventing you from carrying out your job effectively. They may be senior to you, a peer, a parent or a team member who reports to you. The bottom line is that you will want to get them on side. However, you will remember that we mentioned self-awareness earlier in the chapter (and will again in Chapter 10), and *you* may even be perceived by others as a challenging or difficult colleague yourself, so it is always worth considering the impact of your actions on those you come into contact with on a daily basis. With so many personalities and egos involved it is worth keeping in mind that all forms of communication are a two-way process, and if you are finding someone difficult, you should take time to reflect on whether you are always polite to them. The old adage, 'treat people the same way that you expect to be treated' is always useful to remember.

> all forms of communication are a two-way process

---

brilliant activity

This is an activity you can do on your own, but it can lead to effective discussion if done in pairs or a group.

- Think of an encounter you have had recently with a challenging person that you wish had gone better. Consider the reasons why it was not as successful as you wanted it to be.

- Now think about a conversation you want to have or need to have with a challenging person. How are you going to ensure it happens and how will it be conducted?

- How do you normally deal with challenging people?
- What is the primary way in which you deal with difficult people – i.e. do you normally do this by email or directly confronting the person?

For most people, the thought of having to engage in a difficult situation is somewhat threatening in itself. Indeed, there are very few people who relish the idea of tackling an awkward issue. The first, and arguably most important, thing to keep in mind, however, is that the conversation must take place if the matter is to be resolved. Moreover, you will note we use the word 'conversation'. Writing an email or a memo is, effectively, opting out and can have the effect of upsetting the recipient even more and perhaps result in further loss of respect. Similarly, a phone call does not express body language and there can be misunderstandings. In her book *Fierce Conversations* (2003), Susan Scott emphasised the importance of engaging in dialogue: 'Our work, our relationships, and our lives succeed or fail, one conversation at a time.' Essentially, we need to recognise that, if we are to have truly effective working relationships, we need to develop and practise the art of communication.

Having the conversation

Before we look at the mechanics of the conversation itself, it is worthwhile reflecting on the following questions:

- How do conversations normally happen? Are they always planned or do they occur randomly (i.e. in the corridor or at break in the staffroom)?
- What things tend to get in the way when we converse with someone we perceive to be challenging? Is sufficient time put aside?
- How can these types of conversation become more effective?
- What do we need to do to have better conversations?

Initially, it is important that the conversation is *planned* and that both you and the other person have put aside sufficient time. It is also important that both parties are aware of the focus of the conversation. If you plan to speak to someone then do not be vague, as this confuses the matter. Use phrases such as, 'Can we arrange a time to discuss Billy's behaviour?' or 'Can we meet to discuss my timetable?' Try to avoid being too general, such as, 'Would it be possible to talk to you at some point?' Once you begin the conversation, set limits about how long it will be and make it clear that you are not asking for consensus or agreement necessarily – simply to be heard. Finally, try to be succinct and remember that anecdotes, whilst you think they may be entertaining, can take time away from the other person.

Over the last 20 years or so there has been extensive research into the art of communicating effectively, much of it relating to getting people on side, particularly the more difficult ones. It is believed that over 70 per cent of conversations take place without actually talking. Much can be 'said' through facial expressions, hand gestures and body language generally.

> over 70 per cent of conversations take place without actually talking

Nevertheless there are various techniques you can develop that will help you to have better conversations.

1 Pacing

One technique is known as pacing. This is a method used when you want to establish a rapport with the person in question. It is done by matching what the other person is doing and can be done both verbally and non-verbally. For example, if the person is sitting with their legs crossed, you might do the same or you may match the tone and speed of their voice. You need to be careful with this, however; if the tone of their voice is particularly low or high, it would not be a good idea to try to match this, as they might feel you are trying to imitate them and feel insulted! Another technique worth trying is listening to the tempo of people's speech and seeing if you can match it. Again, however, this will not work straight away necessarily and needs practice.

2 *Leading*

This means that you understand when you have matched someone else's pace and you are able to increase or decrease the pace for the other person to follow. A person who leads effectively normally begins by pacing and then leads using the rhythm or tempo of their voice alongside their body language.

brilliant tip

The next time you are in the staffroom or, for that matter, any public place, try to take note of two people deep in conversation. Normally you will see that they are matching each other very closely in body language. For example, if one of them is sitting with their arms crossed this will often be matched by the other doing the same. This is usually even more marked if they are both in agreement about the issue they are discussing. This is natural human behaviour and happens unconsciously. Therefore, the more aware you are of this technique and able to read body language, the stronger position you will be in.

3 *Assertiveness*

In difficult conversations using assertiveness principles to identify your rights and responsibilities can be extremely effective. You have the right to be listened to and to speak the truth as you see it. Moreover, you are entitled for this to take place in a safe and non-aggressive environment. You also have the right to say what you believe to be fair and reasonable in the circumstances.

However, you should be prepared for the other person to be able to say what they see as fair if the conversation is to be of any value.

4   Challenging faulty inner dialogue

When we engage in any conversation we feel worried about, it is paramount that our 'self-talk' is positive. This means we should tell ourselves positive things about what we can do, rather than negative ones. For example, rather than thinking, 'If I suggest this they will think really badly of me', you should be thinking, 'By suggesting this I can make my views known.' Moreover, what we think influences the way we feel and this, in turn, influences the way we behave. If you genuinely feel anxious about something it is your right to mention it without feeling there will be recriminations.

Handling different types of 'difficult people'

The final section of this chapter looks at various types of challenging individual and offers some strategies when dealing with them. You may find that some people fall into more than one of these categories and this will, hopefully, provide you with some ideas on how to handle those awkward conversations. Be careful – you may even recognise yourself as one of these!

> you may even recognise yourself as one of these!

The dominator

This person is always dominating conversations and makes it clear they want to be heard. They have a need to express their opinion and have a better way of doing things. They might have had more experience than you and feel you should benefit from it.

How to handle the dominator

Acknowledge their experience and tell them how useful that might be to you. Avoid telling them that they are wrong. Instead, use phrases such as, 'From my own experience ...' Moreover, seek to use your body language, effectively employing the pacing and leading techniques we discussed earlier. Finally, keep fundamental respect intact and recognise the contribution they can make.

↗ brilliant case study

Sarah was a newly appointed subject leader in what was deemed a failing department. One of the reasons for this was that there was no unity in the department; it was a collection of individuals, one of whom had tendencies of the dominator. She recognised early on that change would have to take place and it would be to her advantage to have the person on side. She had also noticed the person's influence over other members of the department. Whenever she wanted to introduce a new idea, rather than speak to the department as a whole she would approach the dominator first and get their opinion. When it came to sharing the idea with the rest of the department, the dominator would often propose it. Sarah had developed an excellent way of controlling the dominator and making it seem as if the ideas had come from them.

The manipulator

This person likes things their own way and is often negative towards initiatives they might find threatening. Often they may want to change the process and sometimes will distort information in an attempt to put a different spin on things. They are difficult to handle because they appear highly confident.

How to handle the manipulator

Begin by accepting that you may have differences of opinion. Clarify how you feel and your expectations (if you are their boss). Don't 'give in' for fear of backlash, as this is what the person is hoping for. If you are their boss, it is worth speaking to them privately before any meeting to minimise any tension that may occur. Explain to them that you understand there is disagreement between you, and they are at liberty to express this to you, but you would not expect them to voice this during the meeting itself.

The whinger

This person tends to dismiss all new ideas with phrases such as, 'We tried that before and it never worked. It'll never work now.' They are threatened by change and play the victim card. This person is difficult to deal with because they are always negative. A bigger problem can be that they may influence those around them.

How to handle the whinger

Begin by trying to get them to explain why they feel as they do. It is a good idea to ask them to be specific about the issue they have, as this stops them from whining about everything. It can be helpful to assign an individual task to them, as not only does it involve them in the process, but it will also allow you to praise them later. Whatever happens, avoid being dragged down and remain positive yourself.

 brilliant recap

- The ability to manage your emotions is now recognised as integral to any form of success. The most effective teachers are aware of this and use emotional intelligence to bring about improvement in the students they teach as well as their colleagues!

- You are the one that controls your emotions and you must be able to react appropriately in any situation.

- The more aware you are of the workings of the brain the better. You can rationalise things more clearly and are aware of the stimulants that upset you or make you happy.
- Challenging adults are just as difficult as challenging students. Being able to manage them effectively should be seen as an essential part of your toolkit.

Summary

Often it can be the case that the difference between a good teacher and an excellent one is the latter's ability to control their emotions in a variety of situations. Having some awareness of the workings of the limbic system and having the ability to rationalise thoughts when you feel provoked is not an easy skill to develop. Nevertheless, it is an essential one. Additionally, recognising when either yourself or a student is undergoing an amygdala hijack and knowing what to do next will prove invaluable in managing the emotions of yourself and others. Alongside this there will definitely be times when you will have to engage in a conversation you perceive as 'difficult'. Remember, the thought of the conversation usually is worse than the reality. These conversations are essential and work best when you confront the problem rather than the person and remain in control of your own emotions. Whatever you do, good luck and remain positive!

CHAPTER 10

The learning journey

If we wait for the moment when everything, absolutely everything, is ready we shall never begin.

Ivan Turgenev

Frequently in life people fail to achieve their potential. So many times this has nothing to do with their ability or how they are seen by others. Sadly, it is often down to how they perceive themselves and a belief that they are not yet ready to move on to the next challenge. They put off looking for promotion because they have not gained experience in this or that field. Hopefully, you have found this book useful in giving you ideas to improve upon your current performance. If nothing else, perhaps it has confirmed what you already suspected. Not only do we want to encourage you to continue to work towards being the best teacher you can, we want you to inspire and motivate those around you and assist them in their goals as well. We believe that, in order to do so, it is important that you consider your career over the next few years. The aim of this chapter, therefore, is to provide you with ways to focus on your next steps.

Becoming a school leader at any level is an important move and one that brings about new challenges as well as influence over others. It is also recognition for the experience you have gained and will provide you with the opportunity to learn new skills. Finally, it is essential to recognise that there are now many routes you can take within the profession that will enable you to focus on career progression. We will begin by examining where you want to be before considering the options available to you and then discussing the personal qualities required, the application and interview process.

Where are you now?

Whether you are at the start of your career or three or four years in it is important to reflect upon the experience you have banked to date. All of your learning so far will have been useful in some shape or form. Moreover, if you have made mistakes and have learnt from them you will be in an even stronger position than if you had not. As John Bradshaw (an American educationalist and author) noted, 'It's okay to make mistakes. Mistakes are our teachers – they help us to learn.'

The aim of this next activity is to fire your imagination. We want you to imagine that there is no such thing as failure and you determine the level of success that you achieve. In addition, we want you to start seeing yourself in the most positive light you can. In short, we want you to consider the question we have posed throughout the book – do you aim to be ordinary or extraordinary?

> do you aim to be
> ordinary or extraordinary?

 **brilliant** activity

This activity takes no more than 10 minutes and can be used as an excellent tool for making clear your aspirations and the requirements needed to fulfil them. It can be done on your own or in pairs to bring about discussion. Write down on a piece of paper where you see yourself in five or ten years' time. As a subject leader, perhaps, or a year head. Indeed, you may even see yourself as a member of a senior leadership team, either within your current school or elsewhere. Next, jot down the personal and professional qualities you think are required to perform successfully in this post. These may include things like self-awareness, communication skills, ability to analyse data, etc. Now consider how you are going to go about closing the gaps. For example, is there the opportunity in your school to 'shadow' a colleague and to experience what is involved on a day-to-day basis? What type of INSET is available to you? Some schools run what are known as 'Twilight' sessions after school, in which staff in differing positions share their expertise. The task for you is to begin your learning journey.

Progression within the classroom

Over the last decade or so greater recognition has become available for teachers who can demonstrate how they have developed their classroom practice. Apart from seeking promotion in the traditional manner, such as head of department or head of year, a variety of opportunities beginning with the 'Threshold' (upper pay spine) are open to you. Figure 10.1 gives an outline of ways to move on in your career without

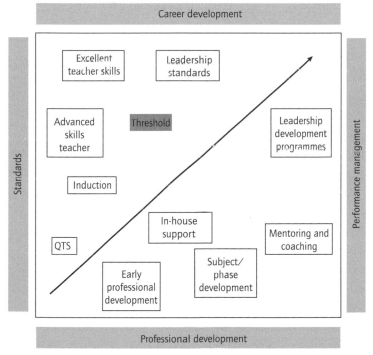

Figure 10.1 Professional development routes

moving out of the classroom. It provides an overview of career progression routes and you can find get a more in-depth picture by going to www.teachernet.gov.uk/teachingand learning/professionalstandards.

Threshold

Allowing teachers to progress to the upper pay spine (UPS1), also known as the Threshold, is intended to reward good classroom teachers who have demonstrated they have met the 10 Post Threshold Standards (see below). Once a teacher reaches M6 on the pay scale, they are entitled to apply to be assessed against the standards, which effectively is worth an additional £2,000 to their salary. The majority of those who apply for the Threshold are successful and it is a key way for schools to encourage continuing professional development.

Post Threshold Standards

P1 – Contribute significantly, where appropriate, to implementing workplace policies and practice and to promoting collective responsibility for their implementation.

P2 – Have an extensive knowledge and understanding of how to use and adapt a range of teaching, learning and behaviour management strategies, including how to personalise learning to provide opportunities for all learners to meet their potential.

P3 – Have an extensive knowledge and well-informed understanding of the assessment requirements and arrangements for the subjects/curriculum areas they taught, including those related to public examinations and qualifications.

P4 – Have up-to-date knowledge and understanding of the different types of qualifications and specifications and their suitability for meeting learners' needs.

P5 – Have a more developed knowledge and understanding of their subjects/curriculum areas and related pedagogy, including how learning progresses within them.

P6 – Have sufficient depth of knowledge and experience to be able to give advice on the development and well-being of children and young people.

P7 – Be flexible, creative and adept at designing learning sequences within lessons and across lessons that are effective and consistently well matched to learning objectives and the needs of learners and which integrate recent developments, including those relating to subject/curriculum knowledge.

P8 – Have teaching skills which lead to learners achieving well relative to their prior attainment, making progress as good as, or better than, similar learners nationally.

P9 – Promote collaboration and work effectively as a team member.

P10 – Contribute to the professional development of colleagues through coaching and mentoring, demonstrating effective practice and providing advice and feedback.

Excellent Teacher Scheme

This offers teachers the opportunity to gain further recognition for their teaching skills once they have reached the top of the upper pay scale. It is intended primarily for those who do not wish to move into a management role and are looking to assist others in developing their teaching skills. Excellent Teachers operate in their own school and are recognised as excellent practitioners. In order to achieve Excellent Teacher status, teachers need to undergo an assessment process that allows them to contribute to the professional development of colleagues in the school in which they teach. As with the Threshold, there are a variety of standards to demonstrate and these can be found on the Teachernet website, mentioned previously.

Advanced Skills Teachers

Also known as ASTs, these are teachers who want to go one step beyond the Excellent Teacher Scheme and develop teaching and learning in their own schools and other schools in the local area. ASTs usually spend 80 per cent of their time in their own school and the other 20 per cent assisting colleagues elsewhere. ASTs are expected to carry out a range of tasks including:

- providing 'model' lessons to demonstrate best practice;
- leading the professional development of colleagues;
- supporting the induction of new teachers;
- supporting colleagues who are failing to secure high standards;
- advising colleagues on issues of teaching and learning generally.

In order to qualify as an AST, teachers need to meet 28 standards, including those required for the Excellent Teacher Scheme. Once again, these standards can be found on the Teachernet website. Finally, potential ASTs must meet with an external assessor who judges the application against the criteria. Notification is given on the same day as to whether the applicant has succeeded or not.

Hopefully, you will decide to stay in the classroom and seek to improve both your own skills and those of your colleagues. However, it must be made clear that all of the above require you to demonstrate evidence of having met the standards. Sometimes this can be in the way of interviews with colleagues who have worked with you, students or parents, but most often it is in the way of records you have kept or can locate with little difficulty. Teachers who have trained within the last five years or so will be used to this type of evidence collection and should not feel intimidated by it, though it is worth checking with the person responsible for professional development in your school before proceeding.

Personal qualities

With any position in any organisation there are a variety of personal qualities needed to be successful. Being a leader at any level in a school is no different. It is essential to recognise that, because of the nature of the organisation (i.e. it is people-based), you need to be able to take colleagues with you.

brilliant activity

Consider the career route you might want to take. It might be departmental or pastoral (i.e. subject leader or head of year). For the purposes of this activity it does not matter too much, as long as you have something in mind. For example, in any leadership role it is inevitable that, at various stages, colleagues will question your decisions. This is not a bad thing in itself and all leaders need to reflect upon what they do, as long as the person questioning is doing it for the right reasons. As a leader you will need to be able to justify your decisions and have the courage of your convictions. Below is a list of 10 qualities that are essential for any leader. Consider which qualities you think you have and which you most need to develop.

- *Self-awareness.* Knowing how you are perceived by others and the impact of your actions on those around you is important for any leader. This, in essence, is being able to hold a mirror up to yourself, having an understanding of your strengths and weaknesses.

- *Humour.* Being able to laugh at situations not only relieves stress, but is actually a quality of effective leadership. The best leaders know when to use humour to effect and have the ability to laugh at themselves.

▶

- *Empathy*. Excellent leaders are able to put themselves in the positions of others and see things from their points of view. It might not make the leader change their decision, but it gives them another perspective.

- *Listening skills*. Every leader must be a good listener. This means not just hearing what others are telling you, but also actively listening. Good leaders show that they are listening through facial expressions and body language. The very best leaders make the speaker comfortable through nodding at appropriate moments, making eye contact and using questioning to clarify what is being said. In essence, they listen with their hearts by giving 100 per cent attention.

- *Approachability*. Being someone who others can share problems or ideas with is an integral part of leadership in today's world. It does not mean people will see you as 'soft', but that they are confident enough to trust that you will listen and advise them accordingly.

- *Communication skills*. The skill of communicating to a range of audiences is important to any school leadership post. Whether this be students, other colleagues, parents or governors, an ability to get your message across is vital.

- *Ability to delegate*. All effective leaders recognise that they cannot do everything themselves and also see delegation as an opportunity to develop others. However, delegating the right job to the right person is an important skill in itself.

- *Vision*. Being able to visualise where you see the team in the future and how you intend to get there is a major attribute for any leader. Having the ability to share this with the rest of the team and take them with you is just as important.

- *Organisational skills*. An ability to be highly organised is important in getting things done. This means ensuring tasks are completed on time and delegating effectively. It also means planning ahead so that any mishaps do not leave you exposed.

- *Resilience*. At times things will get tough and self-doubt may creep in. This is when leaders need to believe in themselves and keep going. Having the capacity to accept criticism and bounce back is a requirement of any leader.

Again, this is something that can be done with a colleague. The important thing to take on board is that *all* of these are essential qualities and will need to be used at different times for differing purposes. It might well be at the moment that you are someone who is very popular and everyone feels they can talk to you about anything, but that might also mean that much of your time is taken up with other people's problems at the expense of other areas of your work. Moreover, being able to hand responsibility to others is not just important in terms of ensuring everything gets done, but also because it allows others to see that you trust them and are willing to invest in their professional development. In short, the most effective leaders are able to recognise and accept their areas of personal development and actively seek ways to improve upon them.

> *all* of these are essential qualities

brilliant tip

If you really want to find out how others perceive your strengths and weaknesses, why don't you ask them? By designing a questionnaire with the 10 personal qualities already discussed you can ask colleagues to rate you on a 1–4 scale (1 = excellent, 2 = good, 3 = satisfactory and 4 = poor). The best way of doing this is by inviting at least five colleagues to give you feedback. Additionally, try to ensure they are not all in the same department or scale as you. For example, if you are in your third or fourth year of teaching, you might want to include a newly qualified teacher, a middle manager and a senior teacher in your sample. If you want to ensure useful feedback, make sure that as many of the questionnaires go to colleagues who you *know* will give you honest feedback.

Essentially, much of your professional development will depend on how seriously you take it. The National College for Leadership of Schools and Children's Services has developed courses that you can tailor to your individual needs. These include 'Leading From the Middle' and 'Leadership Pathways', which are designed for middle and senior leaders. As well as speaking to the person responsible for professional development in your school, see the website www.nationalcollege.org.uk.

The application process: when will I be ready to apply for promotion?

There are no easy answers to this question. It used to be believed that you should not even consider applying for a post as head of department or head of year until you had at least five years' experience. At the other end of the scale, it is not uncommon these days to see people promoted to management posts within two or three years of starting their careers. However, there are two very important considerations you need to keep in mind before applying for any post. First, you might be one of those people who feel you can never move on until you have achieved a certain level of success or have had a variety of experiences. The truth is, however, that this may never happen. As the Turgenev quote at the beginning of the chapter points out, if you wait until everything is in place you will never move on. On the other hand, it is a mistake to seek promotion purely for ambition and, though this may not be as widespread as it appears, you do come across leaders who lack people skills and it is clear they have one thing in mind – getting to the top. The reality is that, when promoted to a management post, you will continue to be subject to the performance management process and oversee it for others. As there are the core standards there are also subject leader expectations that you will be required to meet.

> it is a mistake to seek promotion purely for ambition

Often gut feeling is a good indicator of when you are ready to move on. People 'just know' that the time is right. Others are motivated by the belief that they could do the job just as well as their bosses. In short, it is important that you experience a variety of situations before you consider applying for any management posts and you keep a record of any INSET attended.

 **activity**

Banking experiences

Throughout your career to date you will have taken part in a variety of duties and activities that will stand you in good stead for any future promotion. It is important that you begin to recognise what these experiences are and are able to use them to sell yourself to any future employer. Let's take a minute to consider what kind of experiences are helpful. As well as the ideas below you can add your own ones, which will aid any future applications.

- Team teaching.
- Cross-curricular links you have made.
- All typos of INSET you have attended and have led.
- Involvement in whole-school projects.
- Pastoral roles.
- Outside experiences (i.e. family commitments, hobbies, etc.).
- Assemblies.
- Any coaching and mentoring you may have been involved in.
- Colleagues you may have shadowed.
- Any extra-curricular activities you have been involved in.

On any application form, and during the interview process, it is important to be able to give specific examples of your experiences. The more you can offer concrete evidence of past successes, the better chance you stand of getting the job!

The application process: how to avoid the elephant traps

It is often the case that people do not get the jobs they want not because they cannot do them, but because they have not thought in enough depth about the application process and the planning that should go into it. This section is designed to offer you some tips relating to the key things to keep in mind throughout the application process and interview.

- *Read all relevant information about the post.* You should do your research thoroughly before applying. This includes reading the most recent Ofsted report on the school, as well as looking at the exam results and the specifications and topics studied in the department. Most job applications come with a variety of sources of information, including the school prospectus and newsletters. It does not look good if you seem unaware of the successes or key areas of development in the school or department.

- *Consider whether there is a sense of 'fit' between yourself and the school.* It is a good idea to visit the school if you can before applying. This is a common feature nowadays and can create a favourable impression when it comes to shortlisting for the job. Moreover, when writing your letter of application it is impressive if you can refer to something you have seen in action at the school. The other reason to do so is to see if you can see yourself working there in a management position. Talking to the current postholder and members of the team will give you some insight into how things are done. Often you will get a feel for a place and can tell by your 'gut feeling' whether it is a job you want or not.

● *Consider whether you want to take on the job description as specified.* If there are elements of the job requirement that you are unsure of, or want further clarification on, it is important to ask about these as early as possible. There may be room to do this during the interview itself, but you must ask yourself whether you would be happy doing the job specified. For example, if you are seeking a post as head of history, but the post you see advertised is head of history and citizenship, you may well be asked to teach a large proportion of your timetable on citizenship, as well as being responsible for the results. The question is, will you be happy doing this? On the other hand, does the post offer the challenges you might be looking for if you are seeking a senior management post within the next three or four years?

● *Consider whether you are the kind of person they are looking for.* Earlier we talked about your personal qualities. Similarly, with most applications there is a 'person specification', which outlines the type of person the school has in mind. For example, it might cite the ability to analyse data as a key requirement. As head of department, you would be required to produce an analysis of the most recent set of exam results and the action points that arise from this, as well as being aware of current achievement levels within each year group. Being able to see things through and a capacity for hard work are other common features that appear in the person specification. Again, do you fit their requirements?

● *Consider your letter of application.* It is really important that this is thoroughly planned before you write it up. It is generally regarded that the letter should be in the region of two sides of A4. More importantly, you need to fit yourself as closely to the job description and person specification as you can. Providing specific examples of how you have been successful in the relevant areas will help you to keep the letter to the point and focused. This is where the experiences you have banked will come in, as you will be able to cite them clearly. You should make it clear why you want to work in that school and department. What are the unique characteristics that attract you to the position? For example, it might be that the school is a specialist science school and you are applying to be the head of science, or it is an all-boys school and you are particularly interested in tracking the achievement of boys. It is often a good idea to include specific headings in your letter such as 'Previous teaching experience' or 'Evidence of continuing professional development'. This allows you to demonstrate to the reader that you are clearly aware of the key points and have addressed them accordingly. Finally, do not simply cut and paste previous applications as there is nothing worse than the headteacher of the school you have applied to reading about how great you think the school down the road is. This might be rare, but it has been known to happen. All because the candidate has been careless and has not taken the time to go through their application thoroughly.

The interview process: how to make the most of it

Hopefully your letter will have caught the imagination of the reader and you will have been invited for interview. Once again, the importance of careful preparation cannot be underestimated. The fact that you have been short-listed means that you are already in a strong position. However, it might be that on paper there is little in it between you and another candidate. This is where you need to convince the panel that you are the person for the job. The interview questions usually will be based upon your previous experience, knowledge of teaching

> convince the panel that you are the person for the job

and learning, management of change, management of resources (including staff) and leadership.

Prepare for the interview as much as you can

This includes reading over your application to remind yourself what you have said and re-reading the information that the school would have sent you with the application regarding the school itself. Remember to show explicitly that you know the characteristics of the school (specialisms, whether classes are set or mixed ability, etc.). Additionally, it is highly likely you will be asked to teach as part of the interview process. Make sure that any resources you need are prepared beforehand and that you have informed the school if you need to use particular technology. A word of warning on technology itself: do not assume that the classroom you teach in will have an interactive whiteboard. The intention of the lesson is not to test your ability to use ICT (though this may be relevant), but to see how you interact with students and other adults and whether you can demonstrate the characteristics of an excellent teacher – remember that you will be the subject leader after all!

Prepare your answers based around the job description and person specification

Have lots of examples! Again, this is where your bank of experience comes in. Try to ensure that your response is directly related to the question.

Have a clear model in your mind on how to answer the questions

First, consider what the problem was that you faced (*challenge*), talk about what you did to remedy the problem and what you learnt from it (*evaluate*). Finally, discuss how you would apply your experience to your new school (*application*). If you consistently do this it will keep you focused on the question and ensure that you avoid rambling.

Give yourself thinking time before answering questions

It is important that you think carefully about questions before you answer. There is nothing wrong with asking the interviewer for some further clarification on the question or even to jotting down a few bullet points before answering. Showing that you are thinking about your response is a positive attribute, as long as you do not take too long!

Prepare for their questions and prepare your own

There will be no easy questions at this level, but some will be trickier than others. For example, people often use the term 'zero tolerance' to refer to their approach to discipline. What if you are asked about your opinion of 'zero tolerance'? Is there such a thing and is it possible to apply it in a school? Alternatively, you might be questioned by the students (often the trickiest interview) about what type of animal you could compare yourself with and why. At the end of the interview you will be invited to ask any questions you may have. At this stage it is advisable not to ask about money (you may be able to negotiate this if you are offered the post). Do not feel you *have* to ask questions. If you are clear about what you have seen you can tell the panel that your questions have been answered throughout the day.

 **activity**

Types of middle management interview questions

The questions below are just some of the ones you may come across in interviews. For each one jot down a few bullet points about how you will answer it. You may also be asked to address scenarios. Whatever you do, however, do not assume. With any interview, expect the unexpected!

- Do you regard yourself as a leader or a manager?
- What strategies would you use to instil a shared vision in your team?

- What do you regard as the main factors in bringing about successful change?

- How would you go about tackling underperformance from a member of staff in your department?

- How would you monitor the effectiveness of teaching and learning in your department?

- In what ways would you use your subject to promote cross-curricular links in the school and within the wider community?

- Where do you see yourself in five years' time?

- At a department meeting you are seeking to introduce a new assignment to challenge the gifted and talented students. One of your team seems disaffected and tells you that this was tried before and did not work. How would you respond to this?

- How would you conduct an audit of your department?

- What do you see as your strengths and weaknesses?

- What steps would you take to raise attainment in your department and how would you measure the effectiveness of them?

- When carrying out a book check you notice that a member of your department has not marked books for three months. The colleague in question is a member of the senior leadership team. What do you do?

 brilliant recap

- Consider where you are in your career now and where you want to be in five years' time. More importantly, how will you get there?

- Be aware of both the personal and professional attributes required to make progress in your career.

- Develop a strong sense of self-awareness. How do others perceive you and is this helping or hindering your career?

- Develop your awareness of the application and interview process.

Summary

You need to approach any interview by believing that you are the right person for the job. Arrive with a sense of purpose and self-belief. Whether you get the job or not there is no point in selling yourself short. What education needs at the present time is leadership and you need to show that you are ready to step up to the plate. You should not take a job simply because you are offered it. It may prove flattering to be offered a post, but it has to be the right one for you. Good luck in your career and enjoy your learning journey!

Concluding thoughts

Give me a fish and I eat for a day. Teach me to fish and I eat for a lifetime.

Chinese proverb

We sincerely hope you have enjoyed reading this book and it has given you a greater awareness of what it means to become a brilliant teacher, and also to be one! We also hope that, by following the exercises suggested and reflecting on the case studies, your own practice will have been enhanced and you are ready to move on to the next stage in your career. When all is said and done there is there is no finer profession to be part of than teaching. Education really is the 'silver bullet' and we need constantly to look for ways in which to enthuse those we serve.

> there is no finer profession to be part of than teaching

For centuries those that could afford it put their children through private education and the Brown versus Topeka case in the USA in 1954 highlighted the importance that the Civil Rights Movement attached to the right to receive a decent schooling. Indeed, this was the first issue they tackled. Today we are in a position to provide *every* student with a first-class education and it is our duty to strive to do so. Be proud of being a teacher. You are in a position to really make a difference.

There will always be issues about pay and the conditions in which we work, but ultimately these were not the reasons why we chose to do what we do. Teaching is very much about the here and now. There is no point waiting for the next generation of teachers to address the issues we currently face in classrooms on a daily basis. As Barack Obama reminded us in February 2008, 'Change will not come if we wait for some other person or if we wait for some other time. We are the ones we've been waiting for.' Whatever you do, keep positive and never lose sight of the joy of teaching. Have an incredible journey!

Further reading

[Note: many of the older books are (sadly) out of print at the moment.]

General

Holt, J. (1995) *How Children Fail*. DaCapo Press. (Revised edition.)

McLean, A. (2003) *The Motivated School*. Paul Chapman Publishing. (Challenging and inspirational.)

Wrigley, T. (2006) *Another School Is Possible*. Bookmark Publications & Trentham Books.

Chapter 1 The journey to becoming an outstanding teacher

Gilbert, I. (2007) *The Little Book of Thunks*. Crown House Publishing.

Marland, M. (1975) *The Craft of the Classroom*. Heinemann Educational Publishers.

Chapter 2 Starting afresh: early contact with classes

Wragg, E.C. and Wood, E.K. (1984) 'Teachers' First Encounters With Their Classes', *Classroom Teaching Skills*. Croom Helm.

Chapter 3 A class act: planning exciting and highly challenging lessons

Creber, P. (1990) *Thinking Through English*. Open University Press.

de Bono, E. (1978) *Teaching Thinking*. Penguin.

de Bono, E. (1987) *Six Thinking Hats*. Penguin.

Reid, J. *et al.* (1989) *Small Group Learning In The Classroom*. Chalkface Press. (Brilliantly practical!)

Sutherland, S. (2007) *Irrationality*. Pinter and Martin.

Wallace, B. and Bentley, R. (2002) *Teaching Thinking Skills Across The Middle Years*. David Fulton.

Weber, K. (1978) *Yes, They Can!* Open University Press.

Weber, K. (1983) *The Teacher Is The Key*. Love Publishing. (Both of Weber's books are getting old but still are full of useful ideas and genuinely funny anecdotes.)

Wragg, E.C. (1984) *Classroom Teaching Skills*. Croom Helm.

Chapter 4 Know the golden rules: managing the class effectively

Claxton, G. (1978) *The Little Ed Book*. Routledge.

Olsen, J. and Cooper, P. (2001) *Dealing With Disruptive Students In The Classroom*. Routledge.

Rogers, B. (1991) *You Know The Fair Rule*. Longman. (Everything that Bill Rogers writes is worth reading!)

Chapter 5 Up to the mark: formative assessment

Black, P. and Wiliam, D. (1998) *Inside The Black Box*. Kings College, London.

Black, P. *et al.* (2003) *Assessment For Learning: Putting It Into Practice*. Open University Press.

Clarke, S. (2005) *Formative Assessment In The Secondary Classroom*. Hodder Murray.

Hopkin, J. *et al.* (2001) *Assessment For Learning – A Revolution In Classroom Practice.* Birmingham City Council Education Service. (Video and booklet.)

James, M. *et al.* (2006) *Learning How To Learn: Tools For Schools.* Routledge.

Pye, J. (1988) *Invisible Children.* Oxford University Press.

Spendlove, D. (2009) *Putting Assessment For Learning Into Practice.* Continuum.

Tanner, H. and Jones, S. (2003) *Marking And Assessment.* Continuum.

Wragg, E.C. and Brown, G. (2001) *Questioning In The Secondary School.* Routledge.

Inside the Black Box, Working Inside The Black Box and a number of subject-specific booklets in the Black Box series (English, DT, Geography, ICT, Maths, MFL and Science so far) are published by GL Assessment.

Chapter 6 The data day business: using data for pupil improvement

Pringle, M. and Cobb, T. (1999) *Making Data Powerful: A Guide For Classroom Teachers.* Network Educational Press.

Rosenthal, R. and Jacobson, L. (1992) *Pygmalion In The Classroom.* Crown House Publishing Limited.

Chapter 7 Make it personal: effective methods of differentiation in the classroom

Blum, P. (2004) *Improving Low Reading Ages In The Secondary School.* Routledge.

Cutts, M. (2004) *Oxford Guide To Plain English.* Oxford University Press.

Dickinson, C. and Wright, J. (1995) *Differentiation: A Practical Handbook Of Classroom Activities.* NCET. (The best book on differentiation we've ever seen.)

Gathercole, S. and Alloway, T. (2008) *Working Memory And Learning: A Practical Guide For Teachers.* Paul Chapman Publishing.

George, D. (1997) *The Challenge Of The Gifted Child.* David Fulton.

Ireson, J. and Hallam, S. (2001) *Ability Grouping In Education.* Paul Chapman Publishing.

Lewis, M. and Wray, D. (1998) *Writing Across The Curriculum: Frames To Support Learning.* University of Reading: Reading and Information Centre.

Powell, R. (2006) *Personalised Learning In The Classroom.* Robert Powell Publications. (An absolute mine of practical suggestions.)

Wallace, B. (2000) *Teaching The Very Able Child.* David Fulton.

(See also the Ken Weber books detailed in Chapter 3.)

Chapter 9 Talk to the heart: managing yourself and others

Boyatzis, R., Goleman, D. and McKee, A. (2002) *The New Leaders.* Little, Brown.

Goleman, D. (1996) *Emotional Intelligence: Why it Can Matter More Than IQ.* Bloomsbury Publishing.

Scott, S. (2003) *Fierce Conversations.* Piatkus Books.

Index